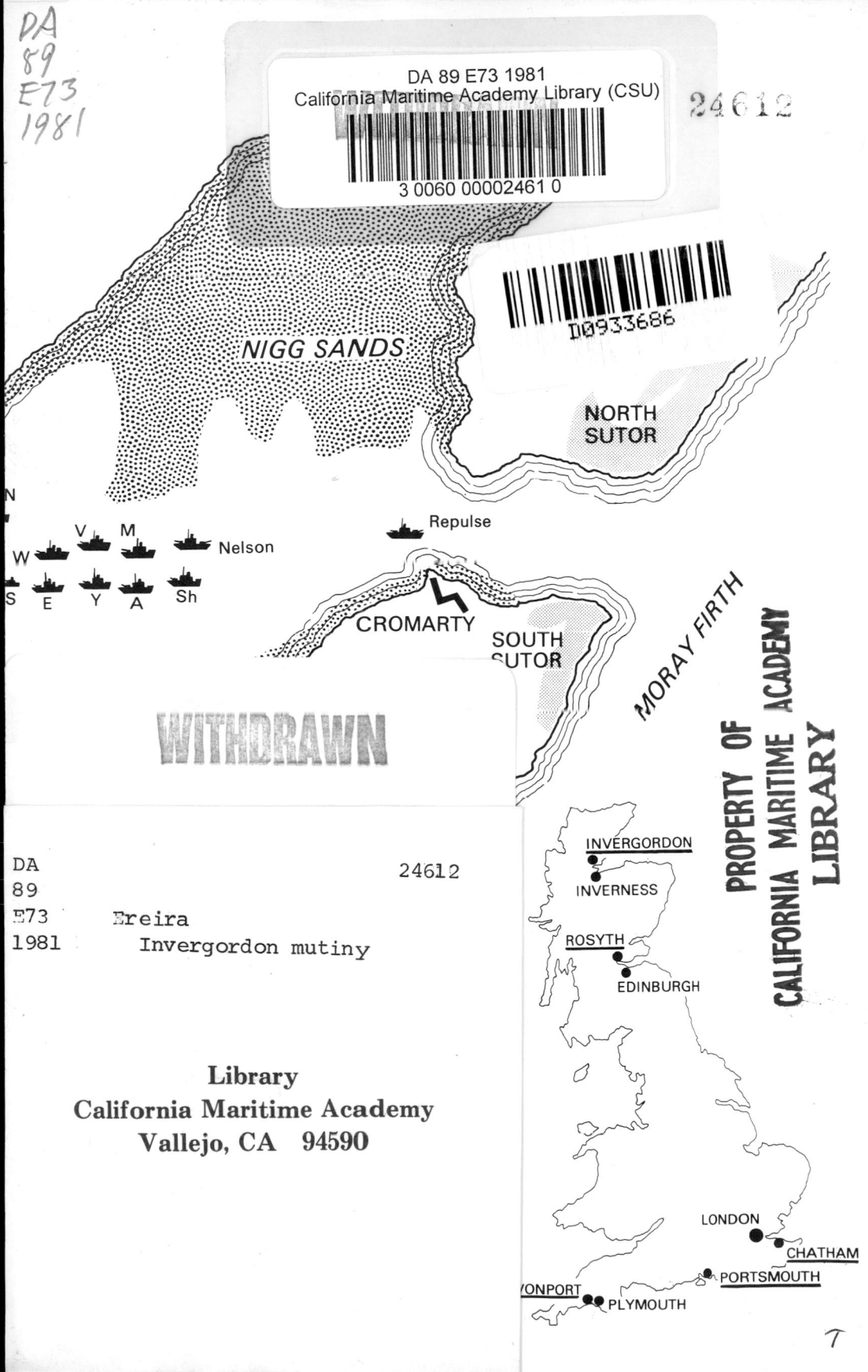

DA
89
E73
1981

DA 89 E73 1981
California Maritime Academy Library (CSU)

3 0060 00002461 0

24612

D0933686

WITHDRAWN

DA   24612
89
E73   Ereira
1981   Invergordon mutiny

Library
California Maritime Academy
Vallejo, CA   94590

NIGG SANDS

NORTH
SUTOR

N

V   M
W   Nelson

S   E   Y   A   Sh

Repulse

CROMARTY

SOUTH
SUTOR

MORAY FIRTH

PROPERTY OF
CALIFORNIA MARITIME ACADEMY
LIBRARY

INVERGORDON

INVERNESS

ROSYTH

EDINBURGH

LONDON

CHATHAM

PORTSMOUTH

VONPORT

PLYMOUTH

T

The
Invergordon
Mutiny

24612

The Invergordon Mutiny

A narrative history of the last great mutiny
in the Royal Navy
and how it forced Britain off the
Gold Standard in 1931

Alan Ereira

PROPERTY OF
CALIFORNIA MARITIME ACADEMY
LIBRARY

Routledge & Kegan Paul
London, Boston and Henley

First published in 1981
by Routledge & Kegan Paul Ltd
39 Store Street, London WC1E 7DD,
9 Park Street, Boston, Mass. 02108, USA and
Broadway House, Newtown Road,
Henley-on-Thames, Oxon RG9 1EN
Phototypeset by Input Typesetting Ltd, London SW19 8DR
and printed in Great Britain by
Hartnoll Print Bodmin, Cornwall
© Alan Ereira 1981
No part of this book may be reproduced in
any form without permission from the
publisher, except for the quotation of brief
passages in criticism

ISBN 0–7100–0930–5

24612

Contents

Preface

As soon as the Invergordon mutiny ended, Paymaster Lieutenant-Commander L. C. Duckworth, in HMS *Nelson*, wrote: 'The only bright spot is the powerful weapon it places in the Admiralty's hands in future when governments light heartedly propose mucking about with the Navy.' A study of the mutiny from the memories of those involved seemed appropriate to the times we live in: it was a mutiny which grew out of a harsh economic climate, with unemployment marching towards three million and with massive public spending cuts being imposed. Britain in 1981 has good reason to be interested in the history of 1931: to see how far the social fabric may be stretched before it starts to rend, and what measures may be taken when the rending starts.

This book originated with an appeal for men who took part in the 'mutiny' at Invergordon to help in the compilation of a radio programme, to commemorate the fiftieth anniversary of the event. To my great surprise, my appeal produced nearly a hundred replies, and it quickly became evident that far more new information was available than could be contained in the scope of a radio feature. My assistants and I have interviewed or corresponded with over seventy men at length, as well as examining a considerable body of documentary evidence, significant parts of which have not been available to previous authors on the subject.

A number of things have emerged which go beyond the straightforward lower-deck account which I had envisaged. One is the startling discovery, from the papers of the then Deputy Chief of Naval Staff, that an armed assault on the mutinous fleet was seriously considered by the Board of

Admiralty. Another is the role of apparitions in the making of history.

There are three apparitions in this story. The first is the spectre of mutiny itself: the collapse of discipline in Britain's largest warships created a shock which still unnerves the Navy. The second is the spectre of insurrection: a fantasy which grew in the minds of the Admiralty and the Cabinet, and which achieved more for the sailors than the mutiny itself – and of which they knew nothing. The third, and strangest of all, is the mystery of Admiral Sir John D. Kelly.

This is not a definitive history of the mutiny; it may be that such a history can never be written. It is, as things have turned out, more of a study of states of mind. What actually happened at Invergordon remains, so far as I can see, a mystery. This is an account of what the people who were there believe took place.

Throughout the text, I have given people the ranks, rates and titles which they held in 1931.

Acknowledgments

Many people worked on the collection of material for this book. Interviews were carried out by Molly Price-Owen, Walter Hall, Alan Cuthbertson, Sean Maffett, Michael Cooke and Mike Hopwood. Thanks are due to Mrs Grace Duckworth for permission to quote from the journal of Captain A. D. Duckworth, and to Commander C. Drage for permission to quote from his papers.

A major part of the documentary research was undertaken by Howard White, and I am extremely grateful for his diligence, clarity and good sense and for his comments on the manuscript. I am also grateful for advice given by Dr Anthony Clayton, Captain Stephen Roskill and Admiral John Bell, and for the help of my wife, Sarah.

I have received valuable guidance from Dr Anthony Carew, from Mr Southern of the Imperial War Museum, Mr Campbell McMurray of the National Maritime Museum, Barry Duncan and Joe Pengelly.

Above all, of course, I am most deeply indebted to the many officers and men of the Royal Navy who took so much trouble to tell me what they knew – some, but by no means all, are credited by name. It is to these people that I must dedicate this book.

Any shortcomings in this book are entirely mine. The truth, I have taken from others.

Introduction

Just north of Inverness two hills squat on the edge of the Moray Firth: the North and South Sutors. Between them, the North Sea breaks in to form at their back a large and sheltered harbour, an inland sea that can hold a navy at anchor in safe, deep water. This is Cromarty Firth

At times before 1931, Cromarty Firth was a haven for squadron upon squadron of warships, the big ships lying in the deep-water channel down the middle of this small sea, the smaller ones – destroyers, submarines, supply ships – moored in pairs up the narrower inlet that leads on towards Dingwall. At the junction, where the sea suddenly constricts, is Invergordon. In those days it was a town that came to life when the Fleet arrived; in September 1931 there were about 1,000 people living in the town, and some 12,000 sailors in the Firth.

The gentle, soft-spoken people of Invergordon had little to offer them. There was one broad street with three pubs on the 'Carlisle' scheme, utilitarian state-owned drinking-houses with poor beer, and an occasional film show in the Town Hall. Most sailors preferred to take their drink in the Naval Canteen, set in the middle of playing fields about one mile's walk through the town. If the weather was fine they could stroll through the broom and heather in the flat countryside around, but the district was more attractive for officers, who could go shooting in the hills to the south, than to sailors who wanted company and entertainment.

Today, Invergordon is growing rapidly. Cromarty Firth is better known as Nigg Bay, home of the oil construction industry that milks the sea-bed. Vast rigs are built around here, and an industrial complex is expanding along the waterside. It throbs with a powerful optimism, as billions of pounds drive through its arteries.

'Sutor' means cobbler, and the story goes that on each hill a cobbler toiled, but the pair of them had only one last. They would toss it back and forth over the neck of the Firth; gods hammering out a destiny, turn and turn about.

In 1931, when the Atlantic Fleet rebelled against government cuts, the economic future of Britain was being put to the last in Cromarty Firth. Today the hammering of the Sutors is louder than ever, and here our wealth or poverty is being shaped. There is a wry irony in the gap of fifty years.

The sailors rebelled against a budget that had to save £120 million. To the government of that day, Cromarty Firth spelled ruin. Today, in the same water, hundreds of billions of pounds are being brought ashore in oil wealth that lay all the time beneath the Navy's keels.

And the ceaseless tossing of the last goes on, change and change about.

1

An Innocent at Sea

In 1931, John Gosling was sixteen years old. He had joined the Navy a year before, after leaving school at fourteen and then pushing a delivery truck round Aldershot. He had known nothing of the sea when he joined up, beyond some romantic notions based on *Treasure Island* and the story of Jackie Cornwall, the boy VC of the Great War. They were notions that compared very favourably with the life that he did know – a life of dead-end jobs and dole queues.

The Navy took boys like this and moulded them to its own pattern. Each of the three home ports – Devonport, Portsmouth and Chatham – had its own training school, and young Gosling went to the Portsmouth establishment, HMS *St Vincent*.

> What that was, I had no idea. I got off the train at Gosport and stood lost in a void. 'Are you Gosling?' It was a smart looking boy in a white duck suit and highly polished boots topped with gaiters. I said yes, and felt that I was no longer lost.
> 'Where's your luggage, boy?'
> 'Haven't got any.'
> 'Right, I am Instructor boy Meadows and you are late about turn quick march!'

HMS *St Vincent* turned out to be a row of buildings, a large open space and a mast. Gosling was identified to a Regulating Petty Officer, and then taken off to be reborn.

> 'Strip off', said Meadows. At first I was at a loss and just stood there uncertainly. 'Your clothes, boy, you

have to take a shower and don't be all night about it or you won't get any supper.' I stripped off to my under-clothes and stood there embarrassed. I had never stood naked in public before. Meadows looked at me rather impatiently and then with an unexpected note of sym-pathy in his voice said, 'You'll get used to it, so off with them and into the shower.' I had never seen a shower before.

He was told to dress in a long scratchy flannel vest and bell-bottomed blue trousers, and make a bundle of his own clothes.

I never saw them again, though years later my mother told me that a week after I left home for the first time, she received a parcel containing the pathetic relics of my civilian life.

Then began a life of strict discipline, hard work, decent food and thorough-going cleanliness. Every minor piece of slackness earned a whack round the buttocks with the chain of the Regulating Petty Officer's whistle. The first job every boy had to learn was how to use a needle and thread, to stitch his name into his blanket and clothing.

Having become an expert with a needle and cotton our group were now lectured first of all with the 'Articles of War', KRs & AI, short for the King's Rules and Admir-alty Instructions, which were to govern every aspect of our lives from now on. At the end of the lectures all I could remember was one phrase that every regulation seemed to finish with: 'Every person subject to this Act shall suffer death, or such punishment as is hereinafter mentioned.'

Much more impressive and to the point were the regulations of HMS *St Vincent*. These were very com-prehensive and you could be punished for everything except breathing. Smoking was absolutely forbidden and punishable by six to twelve cuts of the cane. Walking on the polished floor with shoes, boots or slippers was an offence. Stealing, losing or mislaying anything was punishable. Being improperly dressed, dirty, untidy, being late, being early, talking or reading in bed was punishable. There was also a peculiar crime called silent contempt. If you looked at a superior in such a way as could be construed as contemptuous, you were for it.

They were taught drill and were punished, and scrubbed the 'deck' and were punished, played sports and were punished, and gradually learned how to look after themselves and how to avoid getting into trouble. By the time John Gosling left his training school, he knew exactly what he needed to know – how to carry out his allotted duties, how to keep himself and his record as clean as a whistle, and how to obey. 'They say walk to the edge of the cliff, and if they don't say "Halt!" you walk over.'

At the end of May 1931, young Gosling was drafted to HMS *Valiant*, where he found life considerably easier than in *St Vincent*. *Valiant* was a battleship from the Great War, fully two hundred yards long and carrying well over a thousand men and boys. Gosling was in a mess-deck with some sixty other boys; they were not allowed to mix with the men, or even to speak to them, for their moral protection. 'This, of course, was impossible to enforce.' Smoking was still not allowed, but was not a flogging offence, and boys were not caned as they had been in *St Vincent*.

The day began at five in the morning, when the boys were called to muster on the quarter deck with their lashed hammocks. Life on board ship was cramped, with all the seamen living and sleeping in the fore-part of the vessel, slinging their hammocks where they could on the mess-decks allocated to them. The boys had to rise, lash up their hammocks with the regulation seven turns of rope, and then struggle down the entire length of the ship below decks, carrying this sausage-shaped bundle on their shoulders. As they ducked and wove under the sleeping sailors they hoped not to bump them and call down curses on their heads. Once they had made their way aft, they emerged onto the quarter deck (officers' territory, always to be saluted, always to be crossed 'at the double' – i.e. running), where the bundle was inspected. If the lashing was not precisely spaced, they had to take it back below, stagger back to their own mess, remake the lashing and start again.

After inspection came a wash and a cup of hot, thick cocoa, and then the boys had to get out hoses and brushes to scrub the decks before the men turned to at six o'clock. They worked in bare feet; adult seamen had the privilege of wearing seaboots and stockings.

On Tuesday 15 September 1931, *Valiant* was anchored in Cromarty Firth, by the small town of Invergordon. The whole of the Atlantic Fleet had come north for its 'autumn cruise', which began with exercises off the Scottish coast. The great majority of the smaller ships were in Rosyth, a hundred and fifty miles to the South. That was altogether a more congenial place, close to the pleasures of Edinburgh. Invergordon was a very small town with little entertainment apart from a naval canteen, and boys were not allowed shore leave to go there. Each autumn, the remote isolation of Cromarty Firth was broken by the arrival of the largest ships of the Fleet.

This morning *Valiant* was due to begin firing practice. Two other battleships, *Warspite* and *Malaya*, had sailed the day before; *Valiant* was due to go out at eight o'clock.

The fire-power lying in Cromarty Firth could shatter any force then known. By international treaty (the Washington Disarmament Treaty) no ships more powerful could be built. *Valiant* was by no means the most powerful of them – that privilege probably belonged to the flagship of the fleet, *Nelson*, and her sister ship, HMS *Rodney*. These were the largest battleships in the world. They were originally designed to be even larger, but the disarmament treaty came into force while they were being built and they were sawn off short at the after end. One-eighth of a mile long, these ships sat low and squat in the water with their bridges set well back and nine 16-inch guns facing forward. Their ugly design, and the sense of immovable fortress power, gave them a chilling air. It was hard to imagine the force that might cripple these monsters. 'We can comfortably accommodate six torpedoes,' explained an officer of the *Nelson* to an enquiring visitor.

The guns could throw a one-ton shell twenty miles, and the ships were heavily armoured floating batteries. The recoil of the guns was shattering, smashing anything on board which had not been secured – recent firing trials had shown that if the guns were fired straight ahead the shock did intolerable damage to the bridge. Even firing at the most comfortable angle meant considerable damage below, and the guard-rails on deck had to be taken down or they would be knocked over. The recoil from a broadside tilted a ship in the water, enabling the next broadside to gain a greater range. This trick could be performed one more time, but a fourth broadside would cause the ship to turn turtle. *Valiant's* big guns were fifteen inches, not much smaller than *Nelson's*, and the recoil was almost as devastating, but for these firing trials smaller, lighter shells were to be used, to save money, and the effect on the ship would be less drastic.

Alongside Invergordon's naval jetty was moored the battlecruiser *Hood*, fully a hundred and fifty feet longer than *Nelson* and *Rodney*. *Hood* was built before the disarmament treaty, without constraints on size or cost. There had been a long argument over the relative merits of battleships and battlecruisers; a battleship was heavily armoured but slow and cumbersome at sea, while a battlecruiser sacrificed armour for speed and manoeuverability. The designers of the *Hood* resolved the problem by making the ship so powerful, and giving it such massive engines, that it was able to move with speed and grace while carrying full battleship protection and eight 15-inch guns.

There were also three of the world's most up-to-date cruisers, *Norfolk, York* and *Dorsetshire*, all on their first term in commission and each almost as long as *Valiant*, though slimmer and more lightly armed. *Nelson, Rodney* and *Hood* were due to follow *Valiant* to sea this morning, and the cruisers would go out next day.

It was Gosling's job to go round calling out the hands at six o'clock. It was then that he discovered that there was something amiss.

> I was amazed to find nobody turning out. To me, that was like the sea drying up. I went back to the quarter deck and I told the officer of the day, 'Nobody's turning out!' He said, 'Well, go round again.' So I went round again, and of course nobody turned out. And then, of course, the Petty Officers went round the ship and said, 'Come on, lads, you've got to turn out some time.' And eventually people did turn out. But that was all. They didn't turn to. When they piped 'Hands Scrub Decks' and things like that, they didn't turn to for that.

The *Valiant* had gone on strike.

The ship was moored to two anchors, and getting ready for sea was a rather complicated manoeuvre. The anchor cables were massive chains, joined together under water with a great swivel. This allowed the ship to swing with the tide, but held it in a reasonably constant position so as not to get in the way of other ships as they swung. To unmoor, this shackle had to be hauled on board and removed, and one of the anchors brought up. The men who were supposed to do this work refused to obey orders, and so the Petty Officers, midshipmen and boys were called on to do it instead. They were supervised by the Signals Officer, Lieutenant-Commander Charles Drage. Drage was, as it happened, an academic expert on mutinies; three years before, he had given a lecture at the Military Staff College on 'Some Modern Naval Mutinies'. He now had the opportunity to make a first-hand study of his subject.

Unmooring the ship and bringing it to single anchor was

heavy physical work; while the boys and Petty Officers struggled, a crowd of men stood watching. They were gathered behind the breakwater that provided some protection from heavy seas when the ship was under way; they shouted comments but remained, in Drage's words, 'punctiliously respectful towards the officers' (Diary, 15 September, Drage Papers). Eventually the job was done, and Drage went aft to report to the Captain: Gosling waited:

> There was a lull in proceedings, and in that lull I sat on the cable, because I was tired. The moment I sat on the cable the rest of the ship's company just flooded onto the forecastle and sat on the cable, just like that.

The ship was immobilised. The time was about seven-thirty. At eight o'clock, on every ship, the Garden Band of the Royal Marines began to play the National Anthem. The men sitting on the cables got up and stood to attention while the band played and colours were hoisted. Then they gave a great cheer, which was taken up by each ship in turn down the length of the line.

John Gosling had become an unwitting participant in the largest mutiny in modern British history, and he could not help recalling the very core of his naval training, the lines so often repeated in King's Rules and Admiralty Instructions: 'Every person subject to this Act shall suffer death, or such punishment as is hereinafter mentioned.'

2
The Men

When the social structure of a country is shaken, the breakdown of discipline is more rapid and more complete in the Navy than ashore.

Lieutenant-Commander C. Drage,
'Some Modern Naval Mutinies', Conclusion

The sailors, stokers and marines who were at Invergordon do not describe their action as a mutiny – they call it a strike, or passive resistance. One is a term that describes an industrial dispute, the other more commonly describes political protest; it is interesting that the terms seem interchangeable to the men involved.

In the strict legal terminology, it was a mutiny: as Lieutenant-Commander Drage now says,

It's a nice thing to say that it wasn't a mutiny, and I could say that nobody disobeyed my orders, every single seaman saluted smartly, doubled away, then didn't do what I said. Nobody ever *refused* to obey orders. But the Fleet didn't sail. You can't argue about that. It was a mutiny.

It was, however, a mutiny in which there was no conflict between officers and men. The spirit of the affair is captured in a story Drage tells of the moment when his forecastle party of boys were struggling with the cable. Drage was a new-made father: his daughter had been born just five days earlier.

The sailors were standing abaft the breakwater and looking on, except for one remarkable moment when three of them climbed over the breakwater, marched up to me, put their hats straight and said, 'Sir, a signal has been intercepted. Your wife and daughter are doing very well.' Having said that, they saluted again and renewed the mutiny.

The enmity was not between the officers and the men, but between the Navy and the Admiralty, the seamen and the government. Yet it was born out of social tensions which were threatening to erupt into class war, and those tensions were well represented inside the ships.

Britain in the 1920s was still divided into Disraeli's 'Two Nations', and they knew very little of one another. Hugh Morris, who joined the Navy in 1929, was a boy from the superior nation – the nation of officers and gentlemen, the nation that kept servants and motor cars. His grandfather had been 'something in the City', making his money by trading in commodities which he never saw. It was a way of life which had almost nothing in common with that of John Gosling's world. But both Morris and Gosling had joined the Navy as a refuge from the financial blizzard which was howling through Britain, and which was threatening the very stability of society.

Hugh Morris's father depended on private means for his income, and like many others he suffered from the government's efforts to force the pound to a high value and keep it there. The object of this policy was to avoid the perils of inflation, which seemed very real after the collapse of the German mark.

Before the First World War, money had really been quite simple – the world's money was based on silver and gold coins, and the British gold sovereign, the corner-stone of the world's money, could be freely imported, exported, bought and sold with the currency of other nations. This system, which tied the value of currency notes to the value of gold, was the Gold Standard. It was, in theory, a system which regulated itself automatically: if the Bank of England began to run short of money, it would raise interest rates to attract gold from all over the world.

The Great War had created financial strains which made the system inoperable; during the war, the export of gold sovereigns was forbidden, and at the end of the war the country was burdened with massive debts. In the spring of 1919 the pound would only buy half as much as it had done in 1914. To have restored the pre-war system would have meant creating very high interest rates to attract gold, but that would have turned the government's debts into an intolerable burden. In March 1919, the Gold Standard was therefore formally abolished.

There was considerable nervousness about the effect of having a currency which had no fixed value, and this nervousness was greatly reinforced in 1923, when the German mark fell from 60 to the dollar, to 4,200,000 to the dollar. This was an awful warning against the dangers of being able to print bank-notes which had no relation to a nation's store of gold, and in 1925, after a period of high interest rates which forced up the value of the pound, Britain returned with difficulty to the Gold Standard.

The effects of high interest rates and a rising pound were remarkable. Anyone who had enough money to buy a house in 1921, and invested the money at Bank Rate, could have withdrawn it in 1931 and bought two such houses with the proceeds – and have money left over. The combined effect of a rising pound and the prevailing rates of interest would have added an average of 10 per cent a year to their investment, in real terms.

But an artificially expensive pound had other effects. It was harder to sell goods abroad. When profits were low and interest rates high, few businesses would invest in new production. A world-wide boom began in 1925, but Britain was unable to share in it as fully as France, Germany and the United States. The basic rate of unemployment was more than three times as high as it had been before the war. Financiers may have profited, but merchants and manufacturers did not, and – contrary to the conventional wisdom – this policy began to take its toll even in Hugh Morris's world.

Hugh's grandfather had been a City merchant, and as trade declined, so did the family fortunes. They moved into a succession of smaller homes, shedding servants as they did so. In 1929, Hugh was fifteen. His family could no longer afford to pay his fees at boarding school, and he was unqualified, so he chose to join the Navy as an ordinary boy seaman. There he saw for the first time what had happened to the other nation that lived in Britain.

> When I joined up I met people who had the option of staying in places like Jarrow, where there was appalling poverty, or joining the Navy. They'd been brought up in really grim conditions, and seen their parents out of work. They had a different kind of poverty from us – I had mental richness, they didn't. They'd worked themselves at fourteen, and lost their jobs. You could see the poverty. It was something I'd not known. I'd read a lot of Dickens and I'd seen the Cruikshanks: these people, a lot of them, were caricatures. It showed in their faces that they'd suffered.

The growing wealth of those with money to invest had not been shared by those who depended on wages for a living. As the value of the pound had risen, wages had been lowered at almost exactly the same rate. In industries which depended on exports, and which were therefore collapsing, the buying power of wages was actually falling. Jarrow was a ship-building town and the real value of wages in ship-building fell by 13 per cent between 1921 and 1929. It was also the industry which had the highest rate of unemployment, fluctuating between 25 and 40 per cent.

Inevitably, ship-building towns were great providers of boys for the Navy; so were mining communities, where real wages also fell in these years. For boys from South Wales, for example, the Navy offered shelter from the economic blizzard – if they could get in. Harold Ackland was one of the boys who joined from Newport.

> There was so many trying to get in, and they was so particular, that if you had a tooth missing or a toe overlapping another they would send you away. But these preliminaries in Corporation Road [the recruiting centre] was nothing compared to the examination you then had in Bristol. Nothing at all. I think there was eighty or ninety of us from Newport and South Wales went to Bristol, and I'd be surprised if there was twenty that actually went on from there to Plymouth. They turned the rest down.

Ackland had been driven into the Navy not by unemployment and low wages, but by the industrial strife which they created.

> I was working for a chap called Giddings, who lived on Chepstow Road, and I was going to be an apprentice. In the General Strike the apprentices couldn't go on strike, so I was painting railings on Chepstow Road and a couple of chaps came along and they threatened, more or less, to fill me in if I didn't pack up. So I went back to Giddings and I told him, and I immediately went over to Corporation Road and joined the Royal Navy.

That was in 1926. The pay of sailors had been cut by a quarter the year before, but that was no deterrent.

Wages in private industry were fixed by the iron laws of supply and demand – as the failure of the General Strike in 1926 clearly demonstrated – but in the public services and the Forces wages were determined by government policy. It came to the notice of the government in 1923 that the pay of state servants was not falling as was that of other workers, and a committee under Sir John Anderson was asked to make recommendations. With regard to the Navy, the Anderson Committee reported that 'The pay of the naval rating was not too low in 1914. It is now too high and in our judgement it should be reduced. . .in correspondence with the wages now paid in civil employment.'

The pay of the naval rating had been very low in 1914, 1s. 8d., and when it was raised to 4s. a day, in 1919, that represented a real increase of only about 10 per cent on the 1914 rate of pay. In the next four years the general fall in prices had boosted the value of this pay by about a quarter, and it was now proposed to wipe out the resulting improvement in the sailor's standard of living. A vigorous political campaign was mounted by the lower-deck, through their death-benefit societies. These were organisations of ratings and petty officers, which had become very significant in the agitation for pay increases in 1919: indeed, it had looked for a while, until the Navy firmly forbad it, as though they might amalgamate to form a trade union. The combination of that ban and the 1919 pay rise had led to a decline in the societies, but now they acquired a new energy from the Anderson Committee's threat to cut naval pay. For a while, their campaign proved successful. In 1924 it was affirmed a number of times, in Parliament and out of it, that the rates being paid to seamen currently serving would not be cut – a promise which was never forgotten, and which would be bitterly remembered in 1931. But in 1924 a Conservative Government was elected which was firmly wedded to the notion of restoring the Gold Standard, and that meant further cuts in public spending. In 1925 the Admiralty agreed to find its share of cuts by lowering the pay of new entrants. New recruits would be paid a basic rate of 3s. a day when they became Able Seamen, instead of the 4s received by their older colleagues, and they would remain 1s a day worse off when they reached the ranks of Petty Officer and Chief Petty Officer. The Benefit Societies had already been neutered by a combination of warnings on breaches of discipline, and the insistence that officers attend their meetings as observers.

Hugh Morris and Harold Ackland were both on the new, post-1925 rate of pay. 'The Admiralty thought at that time that a naval rating signed his name with a cross, as in Nelson's time. They didn't realise that there were intelligent men in the Navy.' That sentiment, expressed by a 'mutineer' from *Nelson*, was repeated again and again by the men who spoke to me. Tom Hiscox, who was in HMS *Rodney*, had perhaps the most telling story of all. His family had served below decks in British warships for generations.

> My old grandfather, he used to say when I used to come home, 'You like the bloody navy, boy?' I said, 'Oh, I don't know, granddad, not much.' He said, 'It still reminds me of the old sailing days, when my grandfather and all them were ships' sailors. Same,' he said. 'But you don't get no hard tack.'

The old diet of hard tack and salt beef had indeed gone; *Rodney* provided canteen meals and even had an electric bakery on board. But it was still possible to compare the life of a sailor with that of his grandfather's grandfather in the early nineteenth century. A ship was still a model of the aristocratic state of another age, ruled by social class as much as by the authority of command and still divided into two totally different worlds – the world of the ward-room and quarter deck, on the one hand, and the world of the lower deck, on the other.

When Ackland joined up, he was sent to the Devonport training school, HMS *Impregnable*. This was not a shore base like HMS *St Vincent*, but a set of floating hulks, where the instructors seemed to cling to the ancient tradition that the correct way to bring up a boy was 'at the rope's end'. That had originally meant frequent flogging and, in between times, the indiscriminate use of a 'starter', a short length of knotted rope for hitting boys because they were there. Since this was, after all, the twentieth century, instructors no longer carried 'starters'; instead, they had short lengths of stiff rubber strip which served the same purpose.

Any notions of social equality that might have been spreading in the union-conscious land of Harry Ackland's fathers had no place in this man's Navy.

> When we got onto a ship the officers were so far apart they were like little gods, actually. Now you see the skipper on a Sunday, when he walked round for his inspection; you had a Divisional Officer, which was supposed to be your father, sort of thing, but to get to him you had to write out a request. . .Say I was in trouble, I couldn't go and approach the Officer without approaching the Master-at-Arms, or your Divisional Petty Officer. And most of these things were in writing. You had to put it in writing. And then they used to hold their courts, or sessions, as you might call it, after Divisions, about half-past nine every morning for defaulters and requests and all that sort of thing.

In *The Wonder Book of the Navy* (H. Golding, 1928), Admiral Earl Jellicoe told his boy readers that 'The old-time sailor has largely disappeared and the personnel of the Navy to a great extent consists of trained specialists, each of whom is an expert at his job.' The ships themselves were the latest products of a highly developed war technology, but the world of the lower deck was still composed of seamen and stokers, living on top of each other in cramped mess-decks. In large ships, there might be four 'Divisions' of seamen, each superintended by the distant figure of a Divisional Officer. A Division could contain 150 men, who slung their hammocks where they could and who had minimal locker space. They ate at mess tables which were suspended from the ceiling and which could be readily dismantled for action, just as in a wooden man-o'-war. They sat on wooden forms. In the 1920s they were allowed the privilege of eating with cutlery and their drinking bowls were replaced by cups, but the first impression of an uninformed visitor would be of an undifferentiated mass of humanity.

Even if the work had changed, there were still many men

on board who had grown up in a world of coal-powered steam ships – even of sailing ships. Buck Donovan, for example, a stoker in HMS *Rodney*, had first been to sea when he was thirteen years old in a topsail schooner. He had joined the navy in 1916, shovelling coal into ships' boilers.

> It was hard work and filthy – oh, a terrible life on the coal ships. From 1926 to '29 I was on the last four-funnel coal cruiser; we were in South Africa and we were paid off in African gold. When I came back I went into a pub and paid for my drink with a sovereign. I put it down on the counter and the barmaid said, 'That's no use!' She thought it was a farthing – never seen one before.

The Navy of 1931 ran on diesel oil, not coal, and the work of a stoker was transformed by the change. '*Rodney* was easy, it was switch-on, switch-off, like chalk and cheese, compared with coal ships. Too damn easy. It was boring. Real boring.'

Donovan was on the old rate of pay, and he received a marriage allowance for his wife and children; he was also earning sixpence a day extra for being a stoker, and another sixpence for having two long-service 'good conduct' badges. But he still had to allocate all but 5s. a week of his pay to his family. The whole of his marriage and child allowance went in rent, and his family was close to the breadline. There was a Royal Navy Benevolent Trust, administered by the lower deck, and he had been going to them for help with his children's clothing.

Perhaps the clearest sign of Jellicoe's new breed of 'trained specialists' was the existence of a new class on board, in the form of the Artificers, or 'Tiffies'. These were skilled engineers who did not fit easily into the Navy's class structure.

> If you asked the rest of the lower deck they would have said we were very snobbish. Well, I think we were the first people to use tennis-racquets on the lower deck – I remember seamen referring to them as 'wanking span-

ners'. But we weren't considered to belong with the officers, although in some cases we were getting more than the junior officers, because of our trade pay and so on.

This is Robert Brown, who was an artificer in the cruiser *York*.

I joined as an apprentice, an artificer apprentice, a tradesman, and I did four and a half years training on the *Fisgard* in Gosport. At the end of the time you do a passing-out job and off you went to sea, either as a fitter and turner, coppersmith, enginesmith or boiler-maker.

Artificers were automatically appointed Chief Petty Officers, but they did not have the normal responsibilities for super-vising bodies of men and maintaining discipline that went with those titles. Equivalent to skilled artisans ashore, they were more ambitious than the normal lower-deck in-habitants, and were acutely conscious of the demoralising bottle-necks to promotion created by the pressure to econ-omise – bottle-necks which blocked three-quarters of Lieutenant-Commanders, for example, from any hope of further promotion. The difficulty of obtaining promotion produced a body of young officers who were so afraid of blotting their copy-books that they would take none of the risks that go with initiative, and older officers who knew that they had nothing more to hope for from their careers. The 'urgent need for economy' affected every aspect of naval life, obliging exercises to be carried out at a maximum speed of ten knots (so that ships could not dodge practice torpe-does), forcing men to hand in the stump of an old scrubbing-brush before they could be issued with a new one, and leading to strictures on the excessive use of toilet-paper.

Many seamen did not mind about these pressures; they simply took life as it came, and served their time. But men with ambitions were fully aware of the implications. Robert Brown had been made forcibly aware of the meaning of the 'need for economy' while he was serving his apprenticeship.

> The economy measures of 1923 were a devil of a shock, when they put a whole class out of *Fisgard*. There wasn't all that much prospect of getting a job, even with a skill. And there were rows and rows of ships laid up, all the way up what they called 'the trot', from *Fisgard* right up nearly to Fareham – minesweepers, destroyers. . .

He shared the concern and ambitions of the officers, but did not belong among them, any more than he belonged in the lower deck.

> Officers considered themselves a class apart, especially the junior officers. You'd get a senior officer, he was a nice feller, but the ones who'd just come to sea. . .well, a sub-lieutenant was showing his bird round and she says, 'Oh, what's there?' 'Oh,' he says, 'That's where the lower orders live.' I'd have liked to have kicked him where it hurt most.
> The officers gave the orders and had a very cushy time compared with the men as far as accommodation went. The Captain would have perhaps a quarter of the available accommodation, the officers would have about a third and what was left was for the troops, and they were vastly bigger numbers. There were nine of us on the *Royal Oak* when I was there, herded into a room about twelve feet by six – no ports, artificial light all the time, very little ventilation. The TB rate among the engine room people was very high.
> There wasn't actual resentment, just a feeling that 'they' didn't care very much. They were remote. You just obey orders and that was that. You accepted it. We hoped to get promotion ourselves.

Officers were indeed a class apart, who entered the Navy

from prep. school and were trained at Dartmouth Naval College. They were selected on the basis of 'character', and were trained to lead. With few exceptions, their parents were expected to pay some £200 a year for their education, which was almost four times the basic pay of an Able Seaman.

Boys who came in to the Navy this way were unlikely to know much about the lives of the ratings, and it is hardly surprising that when they came into ships as midshipmen ('snotties') at seventeen, they were regarded with contempt by the lower deck. There were also men who came in as trainee officers at eighteen, but these too were normally from families who could afford a public-school education for them. In any case, many of the non-Dartmouth recruits became Engineering Officers or went into the paymaster branch.These non-military posts were not the ones which set the style of the Royal Navy: their holders were not el-igible for promotion to positions of command (a fact which many of them resented), and had limited powers of punish-ment. The distinction between the military officers of the Navy and the lower deck combined class and discipline in a peculiarly British way.

> 'Yes, sir, no, sir, three bloody bags full sir. They were a different class, the same class as the Admiralty. That was the real trouble' [Ordinary Seaman, HMS *Hood*].
> 'In those days, caste was discipline' [Artificer, HMS *Exeter*].

This profound sense of class distinction was represented not only by the different accommodation of officers and men, with officers having servants to wait on them and different food in large ships, but also by the physical presence of marines between the lower-deck and the officers' quarters. Marines were the Navy's soldiers, originally placed in ships in case the unwilling press-gang victims of the lower-deck got out of hand. The press-gang had long gone, but the marines had not. Robert Brown knew exactly where the

Navy put his social status. He lived on the wrong side of the marines.

Marines did not think of themselves as being in the Navy: they were members of a regiment, and their mess-deck was called a 'barracks'. Men joked about them being there to prevent the seamen from eating the officers, but no one gave much thought to that aspect of naval life. It was simply an ancient tradition that had never died, just as sailors still wore large square collars to keep their tarred pigtails off their clothing, long after pigtails themselves had been forgotten.

Bert Fordham was a marine in HMS *Nelson*.

> I joined the Marines in 1918, when I was thirteen. As regards being a marine, it wasn't much different from being a sailor. You carried out much the same duties as a seaman and you worked on guns, you worked on deck, you worked on hoisting boats, the main derrick and similar jobs. In one ship I was in you scrubbed deck.

Marines were also on the same rates of pay as seamen, with the same distinction between pre-1925 men, on a basic rate of 4s. a day, and post-1925 men on 3s. But like the stokers, they had not been through the mould of the Navy's boy training establishments. They were very conscious of the fact that they stood in a different relationship to authority from that of the seamen, for unlike seamen they took an oath of allegiance when signing on.

> We were sworn men and the seamen were not. Say for instance when they went for their pay they had to take their hat off and the money was always placed on top of the hat, whereas the marines always saluted without taking their hats off.
>
> We were there as guards, we used to do guards of honour and other similar jobs. And we were there for

a landing party, you could land from a ship as a landing party, go ashore and do actions or anything like that.

Bert had married in 1927, but he had to wait until his twenty-fifth birthday, in 1930, before his wife could receive a marriage allowance. Up until the Great War, the Navy did not officially recognise marriage. Even when the sudden influx of married men began during the war, and the Navy was forced to recognise that it needed to pay a marriage allowance to enable family men to survive, married men under twenty-five were deemed ineligible for the allowance. Bert had also lost his good conduct badge, which would have been worth an extra threepence a day, so that things were very tight in the Fordham household. He increased his income by selling colour photographs, oil paintings and birthday cards to his shipmates, and running a 'dhoby firm' – which meant taking in other people's laundry. Many men ran their own little businesses on board naval ships, especially if they were married men with hire purchase commitments. 'Dhoby firms' required no special permission, but men also applied for and received permission to set up shop during off-duty hours in the various gun emplacements, and there they would run sewing machines or manufacture cigarettes, or set up a dart board for other men to use at a price. Others made pieces of craft-work for sale ashore – tapestry work was particularly common, and young seamen marvelled at the artistic flair and craftsmanship of some of the long-service 'three-badge Barnacle Bills', who would clout them for any cheekiness, but who were astonishingly deft with a needle and wool.

The financial problems of married men were well known among the older and more steady single sailors, because many of them took a turn at helping in the Royal Naval Benevolent Trust. George Hill, for example, was a seaman who had joined in 1919, and by 1931 was Commander's Writer (clerk) in the cruiser *Norfolk*. His main qualification for this post was a brief spell as an articled clerk ashore when he was fourteen, during an exhilarating working life which took him through two apprenticeships and work in a catering establishment, as well as going on the tramp and living in barns and doss-houses before joining the Navy aged fifteen.

> In 1929–30 I served twelve months in the RNBT, on the
> barracks aid, serving out five shillings a week for up to
> a month – six weeks as a maximum – to women, wives,
> who were practically penniless. And for their ailing
> child there was nothing else they could have but a pint
> of milk a day extra for the child. When you realised, as
> I did, the cases that you studied, read, that was dealt
> with by an almoner – I would read what his report or
> her report was – well, you appreciated just what a ter-
> rible state the wives were in. In fact it was so bad that
> some of the landlords in Plymouth gave wives with
> children their dinner on a Sunday free, if they were
> paying somewhere around twelve shillings a week for
> rent. Because, it's probably not appreciated, that mar-
> riage allowance went entirely in rent. And therefore the
> wife had to live entirely on the balance of the money
> which was her husband's allotment. If she got twenty-
> eight shillings a week she could say she'd done well.
> But you ask yourself the question, how far could you
> go with twenty-eight shillings a week to feed, clothe,
> light, heat and all these things? No, it's just not on.

Things were even worse for those who married under the age of twenty-five, and were therefore not eligible for a marriage allowance. As for the men on the new rate of pay – well, anyone who joined when the new rate was introduced would be under twenty-five in 1931, with one good-conduct badge if he was lucky, and perhaps a specialist's badge, a torpedoman for instance, worth another three-pence. He would presumably sacrifice his rum ration as well, which would entitle him to a further threepence, bringing his grand daily total to 3s. 9d. Even if he allotted the maximum permitted sum to his wife – six days' pay a week – she would only receive 22s. 6d. a week. With rents commonly around 12s. a week for two rooms in the home port towns, she would be left with about 10s. George Hill, like many other sailors, considered that normal married life could not be expected to survive the strains placed on it by the Navy.

> I always took the attitude that I couldn't understand why any sailor should dare to take the risk of marriage, knowing the tremendous amount of responsibility that was placed on him and the long periods of absence that he would be faced with. Up to two and a half years, which was the length of a foreign commission, is a long time to be away, and it's no comfort to any woman to know that her husband's been away at sea six months and that a child is ill and she's got no one, truthfully, to turn to. If she can't turn to anybody – well, what can you expect?

1931 was the year George Hill got married.

For men who were so close to the edge of financial disaster, every extra penny counted. Those on the old rate of pay, knowing that they had been promised that they would never have it cut, committed themselves to hire purchase contracts to buy furniture, and insurance policies to supplement their pensions when they left the Navy. Many of them were in debt to tally-men who gave trading cheques that were accepted by cheap tailoring shops: a £1 cheque was paid off in twenty-one weekly instalments of a shilling. (It was a more expensive form of credit than it appeared, as a shopkeeper could only redeem the cheque for sixteen shillings.) Their one aim was to keep out of trouble if they could – that way, they could earn good-conduct badges worth three pence a day, after three years and eight years. After twelve years a man's first term of service ended; if he wanted to sign on again, and he had a good record, he would be allowed to do so. Three more years would bring a third badge, and ten years after signing on again, at the age of forty, he qualified for pension. Any act which earned a critical remark on a man's record could carry a serious financial penalty, and making any criticism of conditions or the way he was treated could count as such an act. As stoker Donovan says, 'You couldn't make a complaint without going to the Officer of the Watch, going on Commander's Report and having it passed on to the Captain. A lot of men were scared to make a complaint.'

If a man did have the courage to go ahead with a complaint, his officer was duty bound under Admiralty Instructions

> To warn him that should there be no reasonable grounds for his complaint he is liable to be treated as having made a frivolous or vexatious complaint which is an act to the prejudice of good order and naval discipline.

It was unlikely that anyone who wanted promotion would dare open his mouth about anything. Promotion came slowly and with difficulty. An Able Seaman who could pass an examination was eligible after two years for promotion to Leading Seaman or 'Killet'. (A killet was an anchor, the badge of a Leading Seaman.) This was a role of some responsibility, for it meant taking charge of a mess of sixteen to twenty men; because the Navy was contracting, there were few vacancies, and men often had to wait six or seven years after qualifying for the post before they were awarded it. In the meantime, they had to have an unbroken series of good reports.

Sam Wheat was a Leading Seaman in the *Hood*. He had been a farm boy after leaving school, but he could see no future in a life where 'the first thing you used do in the morning was milk cows and the last thing at night was milk cows.' He joined at Chatham in 1920 as a boy of fifteen, and went through Chatham's training school, HMS *Ganges*. *Ganges* seems to have been the most enlightened of the training establishments, with a discipline which was strict but not arbitrary or humiliating and with considerable emphasis on sport.

> Discipline was strict, but I never minded discipline. Discipline didn't worry me as long as I believed in the people who were giving the discipline. I gradually started to take an interest in the service, you know, and wanted promotion, and tried to get promotion.
>
> To get that you had to wait a long time, for somebody to die. And you had to get 'Superior' on your documents, or red ink 'Recommended'. Then you jumped other people. So you tried to be 'superior' and you tried to put yourself in that position to be 'superior'.

To shake the social structure of Britain, to shake Sam Wheat's desire to become 'superior' and Marine Bert Fordham's alienation from the seamen and Artificer Robert Brown's ambition to be an officer, would not be easy. The identification of caste with discipline ran very deep. There were always a number of officers who had begun life in the lower-deck they were said to have 'come up through the hawse hole', a hole through which a man on a wooden ship might creep from forecastle to quarter deck. The phrase implied that such a man was an intruder into territory where he had no place. That was a feeling that seems to have been rather stronger among the ratings than the officers. These men were never allowed to forget their humble origins and they usually had difficulty in winning acceptance from the lower-deck. When men were telling me how excellent were certain officers, they commonly added, 'He was a real gentleman.'

But in 1931, as unemployment rose towards three millions and social divisions were magnified by the increasingly brutal demands of finance, the men of the lower-deck discovered a new loyalty which over-rode their respect for authority: a solidarity which led them to use the language of strikers in industry and of political protesters. It was a solidarity which reflected the social tensions outside the

Navy, but which found its roots in the lessons that were taught by the very structure of a ship – that officers and men were in different worlds.

3
The Cuts

It is not easy to ascertain the truth about mutinies.
Lieutenant-Commander C. Drage,
'Some Modern Naval Mutinies', Introduction

Lieutenant-Commander Drage's lecture in 1928 began

> It is not easy to ascertain the truth about mutinies. Accounts of them are confused, contradictory, usually biased and often obviously untruthful. Worst of all, it is frequently impossible to obtain records of any kind. The reason for this is not hard to find. Mutinies are neither pleasant nor creditable events and the commonest desire of the actors is to conceal their participation and if possible forget the episode altogether [Drage Papers].

He cannot have been surprised, then, when after the affair at Invergordon, the Captain of *Valiant* summoned his officers and warned them to say nothing about the mutiny – not even to discuss it among themselves. It might, said the Captain, affect some people's prospects of promotion.

A ship is a very private place, and even at Invergordon, where a large number of crews took action together, no one knew much about what was going on outside his own ship. The logs which were written reveal nothing of what happened; in many cases they do not even indicate that anything of note happened at all. The Captains and Admirals present were subsequently called upon to write confidential reports, but these are often misleading – sometimes deliberately so, sometimes because these officers were themselves isolated.

The Admiralty's papers on the mutiny were – with certain evident exceptions – released after forty years, and formed the basis of David Divine's book, *Mutiny at Invergordon* (1970). There are three kinds of material not to be found in those files. The first is any direct information from the men of the lower-deck: the Admiralty took its information about what was going on there from Intelligence reports which seem, from the evidence available, to have been quite unreliable, and from an account published by the Communist Party in 1931, *The Spirit of Invergordon*, ascribed to Able Seaman Len Wincott. Wincott was a seaman in the cruiser *Norfolk*, and he later wrote the only full-length lower-deck account of the mutiny, *Invergordon Mutineer* (1974). The former work was meant to make a political point: the latter is 'ghosted' and does not correspond to any other account. Neither is much to be trusted. Divine, in the absence of any other lower-deck account, also relied on *The Spirit of Invergordon* for this side of the mutiny.

The other material missing relates to the measures which were being considered to deal with the mutiny by the Admiralty, and to the role played by King George V. The Invergordon mutiny was a major national crisis; it rocked the government and threatened the stability of the state. At the height of the mutiny, members of the Board of Admiralty seriously proposed an artillery bombardment of the Fleet – an action which would certainly have had the support of members of the Cabinet. A few days later, largely as a result of the mutiny, Britain's financial policy collapsed and the government was persuaded that insurrection was about to begin in the Fleet: there was a panic at the highest level.

Dr David Owen, who was Secretary for the Navy in 1969, authorised the release of the Admiralty files on Invergordon; even then, nearly forty years after the mutiny, it was a controversial decision which was opposed by members of the Board of Admiralty. I asked him whether he was shown any documents relating to the intervention of King George V, and he replied, 'There are different criteria about revealing documents that relate to the monarchy. They go in their own papers, so that is an area where there might have been some adjustment.'

My request to examine the relevant documents in the Royal Archives met with a dusty answer from Windsor Castle. 'Governmental archives of the period are now of course largely available for research, but the Royal Archives, which contain the personal papers of the Sovereign, are subject to greater restriction.'

Perhaps typically, one of the most revealing documents concerning the Admiralty's response to the mutiny is a letter arguing for the censorship of a book on the subject. In 1937, Commander Kenneth Edwards published *The Mutiny at Invergordon*, a book which seems to have been based largely on conversations with officers and tends to see the whole affair as a Bolshevik plot. Admiral Frederick Dreyer, who had been Deputy Chief of Naval Staff, wrote a letter to the Board which has recently come to light (Dreyer Papers, DRYR 8/1), listing errors of fact and urging that the book be killed.

The official response to the mutiny was one of concealment from the very beginning. The Admiralty and the government avoided the word 'mutiny' as carefully as did the sailors: they preferred to refer to 'disturbances'. They were worried, above all, at the shock that 'mutiny' would produce in Britain and around the world. The idea of mutiny on such a scale, involving so many ships, was too shocking for anyone to want to say it – or say anything else if they could help it. Two days after the 'disturbances' broke out, the First Lord of the Admiralty announced in the House of Commons that there would be no investigation of what had happened and as a result there were no Courts Martial, there was no Commission of Inquiry. The opposition agreed not to press the government for any details of what had taken place. The leaders of both sides of the House co-operated in avoiding any lengthy debate of the mutiny. The silence was literally deafening, as every scrap of official information was suppressed for nearly forty years. Even now, it is impossible to answer important questions about what happened.

The mutiny became such a sensitive matter because it brought about the catastrophic failure of the government's economic policy – a policy that government had been created to carry through, and which was believed by the Cabinet and the King to be essential to the survival of international trade and to the stability of the state itself.

In 1929 the economic foundations of post-war Britain began to reveal themselves as quicksand. The fundamental problems of old-fashioned heavy industries which could not compete against the rising new industrial powers of Germany and the United States had been made all the worse by the demands of financial 'good housekeeping'. To some extent this had been masked by the world boom of 1925–9: while Britain's economy grew more slowly than those of other industrial countries, at least it did grow. But in 1929 the world boom turned into a slump, following the collapse of the New York stock market.

The immediate impact of the American collapse was helpful to Britain: gold flowed from New York to London for safety, and, as American demand vanished, the prices of raw materials fell sharply. A Labour government was elected in May 1929, committed to conquering unemployment and increasing public spending. But the little wave of prosperity was sucked away by the trough that followed, as the ripples of the Wall Street crash spread and worked themselves through the world's economy.

As the prices of raw materials had fallen, the countries which supplied them could no longer afford to import goods as they used to do. Unemployment rose dramatically, and the National Insurance Fund ran heavily into debt. The new government had raised the rate of unemployment benefit, and made it easier to obtain.

A major crisis of world banking confidence began in May 1931, when Austria's largest bank collapsed. Germany's banking system began to crumble, and in mid-July large-scale selling of sterling began. If the pound was to be defended, money would have to be borrowed abroad – but before foreign bankers would lend, they wanted to be sure that the budget deficit would be eliminated.

On 31 July 1931, the Committee on National Expenditure spelt out the scale of Britain's problems, and the changes necessary if the country was to retain the confidence of foreign bankers and staunch the haemorrhage of gold. The budget had to be balanced – which meant saving £120 million pounds in the year to come. This sum, £120 million pounds, was more than was spent on the police and all the armed services combined: it was more than the total spending on education; it was half of the total spending of civil government in the United Kingdom. It was a very nasty shock.

The Committee – known as the May Committee, after its Chairman, Sir George May – had made the most pessimistic assessment possible of the nation's position, and the cuts it recommended were truly draconian. Taxation, it said, should be raised by £24 million pounds, and expenditure cut by £96 million pounds – two-thirds of which was to be found by cutting unemployment pay.

This was an intensely political report, constructed in such a way as to cause maximum embarrassment to the Labour Government – it was also extremely effective in convincing foreign bankers that these measures were indeed necessary before Britain could be lent money to defend the pound. And if there was one point on which conventional wisdom was unanimous – despite the unconventional contrary arguments of Lloyd George and Maynard Keynes – it was that the pound must be defended and the Gold Standard retained. Without that, a hideous spiral of inflation was thought almost inevitable.

Included in the May Report were recommendations for cuts in the pay of men in the Armed Services. 'No officer or man serving His Majesty', said the repoı, 'has any legal claim to a particular rate of pay.' That was not the view of men in the Royal Navy. Those on the new, low rate were complaining as they tried to manage on their money – the 1925 intake of boys, the first to grow up with the new rate, were now twenty-one, and in many cases thinking of marrying. A few were married already, but, as they could not expect marriage allowance for another four years, they were unable to keep a wife and family on what they earned. Those on the old rate, and who by definition had been in the Navy in 1925, well remembered the promises that had been made in Parliament that their pay would not be cut. But the May Committee specifically recommended that the old rate of pay should be abolished, and that all men should go on to the post-1925 rate.

Inside the Admiralty the Permanent Secretary, Sir Oswyn Murray, worked hard on an alternative plan, by which there would instead be a general reduction in Naval pay of 10 per cent, but there were civil servants in the Admiralty who opposed that. The existence of two rates of pay was an unsatisfactory anomaly, and as the post-1925 men grew older and increased in numbers, it was increasingly awkward to have men doing the same job on different rates of pay. Besides, they argued, a cut of basic pay to 3s. a day would not be as severe a blow as in 1925: the cost of living had fallen by 30 per cent since then.

On 19 August, the First Lord of the Admiralty told the Cabinet that the men of the Royal Navy would accept cuts in pay, as long as they were equivalent to those being borne by other classes of the community. Four days later the Cabinet resigned.

The May Committee report, which became the basis for all discussion of Britain's desperately needed foreign loan, had created a political fever. The whole trend of economic change over the previous ten years had been to strengthen a sense of class bitterness. While money placed on deposit in the banks had doubled in value, the real value of wages had risen, on average, by only 2 per cent a year – and unemployment had shot up from 1,200,000 in 1929 to 2,700,000 in the autumn of 1931. The ever-growing gulf between investors and wage-earners was made manifest in the contrast between the social whirl of the Hooray Henrys and the Bright Young Things with banker daddies, and the desolate appearance of the industrial slums. It was a contrast which was increasingly visible, as the cinema was a mass entertainment, and the social whirl had a particular fascination for cinema newsreel editors.

The King had long been worried about the prospect of a major upheaval in Britain. In 1919, one year after the Bolsheviks murdered his cousin Tsar Nicholas II, King George expressed his anxieties to J. C. C. Davidson. Davidson had come to know the King well when serving at the Colonial Office, and was offered the job of Private Secretary to the Prince of Wales.

> He told me there was a lot of intriguing propaganda going on, and when I said that I didn't think it went very deep, he said, 'They are against the monarchy'. . .The King said that he was extremely worried that the miners were holding these views and that politically they were rather effective.

Reflecting on the King's views many years later, Davidson commented

> I don't think he had the slightest idea what was the feeling of the people towards himself until it came out in the Jubilee in 1935. I think that he was politically rather innocent. He was very right-wing and he knew where his friends really lay, and that the Conservative Party was the King's Party and a radical party was not [R. R. James, *Memoirs of a Conservative*, 1969].

The King was as conscious as anyone that the cuts now demanded – particularly the cut in unemployment benefit, which the Labour Cabinet had refused to accept – tended to increase popular radicalism. On 14 July the Macmillan Committee on Finance and Industry had warned of the dangers of continued deflation, including the risk that it would 'initiate social as well as economic disturbances which leave no part of the national or international order unaffected.'

But those were the policies which were to be pursued. Early on 23 August, Ramsay MacDonald saw the King to warn him that the collapse of his Cabinet was imminent. The Labour Party was the largest party in the House, but it did not have an absolute majority: the King therefore summoned the leaders of the Liberal and Conservative Parties. Everyone, including MacDonald, expected that the final result would be a Conservative government with Liberal support, or just possibly a Conservative–Liberal coalition, but Sir Herbert Samuel, the Liberal leader (who saw the King before the Conservative, Baldwin), argued that neither arrangement could persuade the country to accept a budget which would hit so hard at the poorest classes of the community. There would be much bitterness if the poor were going to suffer in order to appease the power of international capital. The King became convinced that only a Labour Prime Minister could carry the budget without a real danger of class warfare.

When Baldwin arrived, King George therefore asked him if he would serve under MacDonald in a National Government. When MacDonald came late that night to offer his resignation,

> The King impressed on the Prime Minister that he was the only man to lead the country through this crisis and hoped he would reconsider the situation. His Majesty told him that the Conservatives and Liberals would support him in restoring the confidence of foreigners in the financial stability of the country [Sir Clive Wigram, quoted in H. Nicholson, *George V*].

The following day, at a conference of all three party leaders, the King pressed his argument.

He trusted there was no question of the Prime Minister's resignation. . .His Majesty hoped that the Prime Minister, with the colleagues who remained faithful to him, would help in the formation of a National Government, which the King was sure would be supported by the Conservatives and the Liberals. The King assured the Prime Minister that, remaining at his post, his position and reputation would be much more enhanced than if he surrendered the government of the country at such a crisis [Sir Clive Wigram's memorandum, quoted in ibid.].

MacDonald agreed to form a new Cabinet, based on Liberal and Conservative support, abandoning his own party. He was persuaded that it was an act of necessary patriotism. Next morning, the *Daily Herald* gave a different verdict on the new National Government.

This is not patriotism, but acceptance of the dictatorship, not even of a British bank, but of international finance. . .It is the severest blow struck at the rights and powers of democratic government. It is the apotheosis of the power of finance.

The paper continued the next day with the same theme.

It is not a people's Government, but a bankers' Government. . .One of the conditions laid down by the banks is that part of the price for saving the Pound is to be paid by the very poorest people in this country.

August is normally a quiet time for newspapers; it is a holiday month, the 'silly season' when there is usually little news in print and newspaper circulation falls. August 1931 was rather different. The *Daily Herald*'s circulation rose by 25,000 to 1,265,000 copies a day.

Parliament was not due to reassemble until 8 September. In the meantime the Trades Union Congress met and denounced the new government: John Bromley, a Labour MP, gave an eve-of-conference address which declared 'This is war, and I hope the opening manoeuvres of the final war in this country between the working people and the financial interests of unadulterated capitalism, which is robbing them.'

Meanwhile, the new government began drawing up its list of cuts and tax increases. The First Lord of the Admiralty was now Sir Joseph Austen Chamberlain, and he had one week to advise the Cabinet on the cuts to be made by the Navy.

Chamberlain was the son of the celebrated Mayor of Birmingham and elder half-brother of Neville, who was at this time Chairman of the Conservative Party. Austen Chamberlain was sixty-seven years old and a political failure. He had been an unpopular (because pro-French) Foreign Secretary in the last Conservative administration, but he had still hoped to get back to the Foreign Office. Instead, he was offered this job, a job which he had never wanted and which he considered was simply a way of shutting him up. It was not a Cabinet post.

He found himself almost alone in the Admiralty. The Civil Lord resigned on 26 August and was not replaced. The Permanent Secretary had been away on holiday ever since 10 August. Admiral Field, the First Sea Lord, was also away sick. His assistant, the Deputy Chief of Naval Staff, Admiral Dreyer, was on leave, as was the Fourth Sea Lord. Having obtained such advice as he could, Chamberlain decided that the May Committee proposals were nasty medicine, but would have to be accepted even though that might be seen as a breach of faith. Everyone must bear their burden in a time of national emergency.

The opening of Parliament was marked by ugly scenes. Three thousand demonstrators marched to Parliament Square singing the 'Red Flag', waving red banners and shouting 'Down with Fascism'. They were dispelled by a baton charge of over a thousand police.

The next day, Thursday 10 September, Chancellor Philip

Snowden announced his budget. Taxes were being raised more than was expected: beer went up 1*d*., petrol 2*d*. a gallon, tobacco 8*d*. a pound. Income tax allowances were reduced, and the basic rate of tax was raised from 4*s*. 6*d*. to 5*s*. in the pound. Surtax went up by 10 per cent.

And then there were the economy cuts: unemployment benefit was cut by 10 per cent, and a means test was introduced to compel the unemployed to sell their possessions before claiming. State salaries were cut by between 10 and 20 per cent – the larger cut being applied to Ministers earning over £5,000 a year. Police constables were to lose 5*s*. a week, teachers' salaries were to be cut by 15 per cent. And defence spending was to be cut by £5,000,000 including reductions in salaries.

The size of the reductions in Service pay was not revealed except in the broadest terms. Chamberlain had wanted to issue a Fleet Order detailing the cuts three days before the Budget: this was prevented by the Treasury, which insisted that the cuts could not be revealed to the Fleet before the Budget speech. But they were already known to the Navy's Commanders-in-Chief, because a telegram had been sent by the Admiralty 'for confidential guidance' on 3 September. 'For the Navy the sacrifice involves . . .placing all officers and men at present in receipt of pay on 1919 scales on the revised scale introduced in October 1925. . .The new regulations are to come into force from 1st October next.'

The Commander-in-Chief of the Atlantic Fleet, Admiral Sir Michael Hodges, did not receive this telegram; he was on leave. It was received instead by his Chief of Staff, Admiral R. M. Colvin. Hodges was taken sick when he returned to his flagship *Nelson* on 7 September, and was taken straight to hospital suffering from pleurisy. Command of the Fleet passed automatically to its next senior Admiral, Rear-Admiral Wilfred Tomkinson in the *Hood*, Admiral in Charge of Battle Cruiser Squadron. Tomkinson was a small, quiet man, little known outside the *Hood*. He had spent his whole career in the shadow of Roger Keyes, who had asked for Tomkinson as his second-in-command in a series of appointments over many years. He had been made a Rear-Admiral in 1927, when he was Keyes' Chief of Staff in the Mediterranean Fleet: he had gone on to become Assistant Chief of Naval Staff at the Admiralty. The *Hood* was his first flagship, and he did not get her until July 1931.

He was now in charge of the whole Fleet by the accident of seniority over Rear-Admirals French, who commanded the battleships, and Astley-Rushton, in charge of the cruiser squadron. Astley-Rushton, who was only one day junior to Tomkinson, had more experience of command and resented the situation. He was an arrogant, somewhat bullying man who is reputed to have said, 'No-one interferes with my cruisers!' It would have been helpful to Tomkinson if he had been appointed to the temporary rank of Vice-Admiral, but instead the Admiralty simply recognised his title as Senior Officer Atlantic Fleet, and told him that the staff were to remain in Hodge's flagship, the *Nelson*. The Admiralty, plainly, did not see the impending pay cuts as being likely to create any unusual difficulties. Tomkinson was not alerted to them. He probably saw the warning telegram on 7 September, but seems to have taken little notice of it. His immediate problem was to get his Fleet to sea within twenty-four hours, and begin exercises *en route* to Invergordon.

Tomkinson's authority, such as it was, extended over the whole Fleet, but his primary concern was with the battle-cruiser, battleship and cruiser squadrons. They were lying in their home ports, ready for sea. In Devonport were the battleships *Malaya* and *Rodney*, two cruisers *Dorsetshire* and *Norfolk*, and the minelaying cruiser *Adventure*. Harold Ackland from Newport was now twenty-one years old, and serving in *Adventure*; he remembers it as an unhappy ship because of the peculiar and unpleasant nature of its work. Below decks it was laid out rather like an underground station, with railway lines running down the belly of the ship and out of a pair of doors at the back. Minelaying meant attaching mines to trolleys which ran out on these rails; the trolleys were sinkers which anchored the mines to the sea-bed. The nasty part was recovering the mines afterwards; it meant bringing a great deal of muck on board and there was much hard physical work involved. Some men add that it was no help that the ship seemed to spend an inordinate amount of time in Scapa Flow, probably the most depressing stretch of water round the British coast.

Buck Donovan, stoker, remembers *Rodney* too as an unhappy ship, but not because of the work. That was no problem.

> There was conflict between groups of men, cliques. Mind you, you'd never get a stoker and a seaman friends. We called 'em dab-dabs, because that's how they went, dab, dab; dab, dab; cleaning things. It was like that on large ships. Most Commanders would bring a ship's company together, but if he wasn't good, people felt 'To hell with it!' I've forgotten the Commander on *Rodney*.

Stokers had their own mess-deck on every ship and did have little to do with seamen – perhaps because they had not been institutionalised in the boys' training establishments, but joined up at eighteen, they got on better with the Marines. But the distance between different groups of men was unusually great in *Rodney*. Many men remember it as a cold ship. There was a minor outbreak of indiscipline aboard early in the summer, and the ship did not do well in the Fleet's sporting competitions – always a bad sign.

In a large ship it was often the Commander who determined whether or not the atmosphere was cheerful. The Captain was a remote figure, often known as 'The Owner'; he lived an isolated existence in his apartments aft, with a sentry on the door. He did not dine with his officers, or they with him, except by invitation; his main personal contact with the crew was with his servants. The Commander was responsible for the day-to-day organisation of life on board and an active and well-liked Commander could attract strong personal loyalty. No men in the large ships of the Atlantic Fleet felt that kind of loyalty towards their Captains.

Rodney and *Adventure* were to be among the worst-affected ships at Invergordon – but so was *Norfolk*, and that was a happy ship, doing well at sports and remembered with affection by her crew. She too, though, seems to have had a weak Commander. George Hill, his writer, regards himself as having been the Commander's go-between, writing his orders and speaking to the men on his behalf.

Hood and *Nelson*, both in Portsmouth were both undoubtedly happy ships with excellent Commanders, yet they too were seriously affected in the mutiny. *Nelson* was Cock of the Fleet, proudly displaying the silver cockerel that signified dominance in the regatta. Credit for this was universally given to the *Nelson*'s Commander, Atwell Lake, known to his men as 'Lou'. His life had been spent in big ships, and he knew how to make them flourish, turning everything into a contest, investing every activity with competitive spirit. He was not an informal man, as was the Commander of *Norfolk*; he was rather old-fashioned and was rumoured to wear corsets. But he was fair, he understood his men and he appeared to love the ship. When *Nelson* went on a visit to the United States she was painted not with the usual dull grey paint but with luxurious enamel. It was said that 'Lou' Lake paid for it out of his own pocket.

Sam Wheat, Leading Seaman in *Hood*, remembers the Commander of his own ship in a similar way.

> I'll always say we had the most excellent Commander you could ever have, he's the best admired Commander I've ever known or served with, and that was Commander McCrum. He was a diplomatic chap. Morale was quite good; there's no question about it, it was a happy ship, a very happy ship.

Whether a ship was happy or unhappy would make no difference when it came to the crunch. The only way to guarantee that a ship would not mutiny was to fill it with men who were strangers to each other. In Devonport, *Malaya* had just been recommissioned and carried a crew of strangers. The same was true of *Warspite* in Portsmouth, and of *Repulse*, which was in Chatham. It was only the recommissioned ships that would sail when ordered at Invergordon.

Besides *Repulse*, Chatham was the home port of *York* and *Valiant*. *Valiant*, the ship which would first refuse the order to sail, was perhaps the unhappiest ship of all. She had been extensively refitted in 1930, and when she came to be recommissioned she was so filthy that the Commander-in-Chief at Portsmouth refused to accept her into the Fleet. Extra men were drafted in to clean her. The presence of Portsmouth men among the Chatham crew made for edginess; each home port manufactured men to its own model, and they did not get on well together. The crew also found it hard to get on with some of the new experimental equipment that had been installed. Corporal Dyke, the marine, remembers the ship as having had an unusual percentage of defaulters on parade each morning, and 'someone was always in the rattle' (the cells).

During the summer the Commander of *Valiant* was taken sick and the Captain, Captain G. A. Scott, took the opportunity to have him replaced because he regarded him as incompetent. Ever since leave had ended, on 1 September, the *Valiant* had been unnaturally quiet; from having an unusually large number of defaulters, she had gone to having an unusually small number. Her new Commander, with fatalistic pessimism, knew that it was too good to last (Elkins Journal, ELK/2).

By the time the budget was announced, Tomkinson had his fleet at sea, except for *Nelson*, which waited in case the Commander-in-Chief recovered. The rest of the Fleet performed mock battle – Blue Fleet versus Red Fleet. Neither Colvin nor Tomkinson seem to have taken the warning telegram on pay very seriously, and now the officers were totally absorbed in their exercises. The day after the budget, the Paymaster Lieutenant-Commander in *Nelson* listened to the Chancellor's radio speech about the budget. *Nelson* had finally given up waiting for the Commander-in-Chief, and sailed to join up with the fleet at Invergordon. Paymaster Lieutenant-Commander Duckworth seemed to know nothing of the staggering pay cut that was being inflicted on the lower-deck. His interest in the budget had little to do with the money he had to hand out; he wanted to hear about the money he received himself. 'Our pay cut is 3 per cent and income tax raised 6*d* to 5/– in the £'. He commented on Snowden's performance in the speech, 'You'd think all the politicians were saviours of the country for getting us out of the mess we're in – not a word as to who got us in' (Duckworth Diary, IWM).

Snowden had, indeed, been Chancellor in the Labour Government and followed Ramsay MacDonald into the National Government. Snowden had always believed in the importance of maintaining the Gold Standard, and it was partly his insistence on the need for brutal cuts to save the pound which had broken the Labour Cabinet. He shared the view of the economist Henry Clay, who had prepared a note for the guidance of the new government, probably in August:

> If the Gold Standard goes, the trade of the world would be plunged into a welter of depreciating currencies and floating exchanges, in which trades will not know from week to week how they stand or whom they can trust. . .
>
> If the pound goes the currencies of half the countries of Europe will also go. . .Revolution will follow in Central Europe, leading possibly to the triumph of international Communism.

Any threat to the strategy of this budget would be seen, then, as a threat to the pound, to financial stability and to international order. When the government were faced with resistance to the cuts they would see themselves as confronting the possible triumph of international Communism. Any measures were justifiable against that threat.

The world had only just witnessed what sort of measures might be used against a mutinous Fleet by a desperate government. At the time when the National Government was being formed, massive public spending cuts were being imposed in Chile. These included cuts of 30 per cent in the pay of higher ratings in the Navy – a Navy which, as it happened, had close connections with Britain. Its first officers had been from the Royal Navy, and its principal ships were built in British shipyards. The men of a number of ships mutinied, demanding withdrawal of the cuts. Altogether there were some 5,000 men involved: the crews of a battleship, a cruiser, nine destroyers and three submarines. The Chilean government negotiated with them, but as unrest spread throughout the country it abruptly broke off negotiations and launched an armed assault on the mutineers, using bombs, artillery and boarding parties. The last ship to surrender was the battleship *Almirante Latorre*. News of the surrender had come on 7 September, the day Tomkinson was probably shown the warning telegram.

If the British government was going to consider acting like the government of Chile, they would have good reason to want to stay quiet about it for a very long time.

4

The Receiving End

The immediate cause of the outbreak is usually a muddle.

> Lieutenant-Commander C. Drage,
> 'Some Modern Naval Mutinies', Conclusion

Sunday, 13th September, 1931
I went into the Commander's office during Church and saw that something had gone wrong. . . [Drage, Diary]

A sixteen-page document had arrived on board *Valiant*, Admiralty Fleet Order 2239. It listed, rank by rank, the old rate of pay and the new. Drage was horrified: 'A shilling off the Able Seaman's four bob a day is 25 per cent – a perfectly absurd cut.' The AFO neatly tabulated the old and new rates of pay, making it vividly clear that a cut of a shilling a day bore disproportionately hard on the lower-paid men. A Lieutenant-Commander was only going to lose 3.7 per cent of his pay, but for lower-deck men on the old rate the table read:

	s.	d.		s.	d.	
Chief Petty Officer	8	6	to	7	6	per day
Leading Seaman	5	3	to	4	3	per day
Able Seaman	4	0	to	3	0	per day
Ordinary Seaman	2	9	to	2	0	per day

It seems purposely to put the whole matter in an unfavourable light [wrote Drage]. It presents the sailors

44

with a *fait accompli*, although it must obviously have been prepared some time beforehand. It makes no appeal to their loyalty and patriotism, and having been kept completely in the dark we officers have had no chance of preparing the men's minds for the blow. In short, the whole thing is a monumental piece of folly.

Drage's job, as Divisional Officer of the small Signals Division, was to look after the interests and worries of the men under him. The expert on mutinies set about counselling his Division.

I spent the rest of the forenoon working out the effects of the Order for different individuals while the rest of the Lower-Deck collectively leaned over my shoulder and breathed down my neck. . .The most flabbergasted are the 'staid hands', Chiefs and Petty Officers with heavy home commitments.

The Able Seamen were suffering a more drastic cut but were not as stunned by it. Unlike Drage, many of them already knew about the cuts.

The thing I can't understand is this: the cutting of basic pay by a quarter seems to be known on the lower deck before the Admiralty sends signals. It was general knowledge on the lower deck before any signals seemed to be sent around to the ships.

This is Harold Ackland, twenty-one years old in 1931. His ship, the *Adventure*, left Devonport on 7 September, three days before the budget.

There were strong rumours before we sailed, in Devonport. In Devonport we had a place called Aggie Weston's, and The Home From Home I think the other place was called. And the three-badgers, the older-type sailors, were collecting in groups more than they normally would do. They would either go in the billiard hall if there was one, or – you weren't allowed to drink in these places, it was a teetotal place where you had a bun and a cup of tea – but they collected more together than they would normally do, talking. When they were coming off from shore they were saying, 'Our pay is going to be cut by twenty-five per cent.'

Tom Hiscox, serving in *Rodney*, had heard the same story.

Well, I used to live with my grandmother at Camel's Head, see; well, that was just a matter of a spit from the dockyards. Of course I used to get home and my uncles were there, Uncle Len and Uncle Bill, both of whom were in the Navy. One was on the Queen Elizabeth and the other was a Petty Officer on the *Nelson*. They used to talk about these rumours. There was a lot of talk spreading around – you could feel it in the air, when you was on board ship. The atmosphere didn't seem to be right. The tension seemed to be there. Everybody seemed to be looking at each other.

Those who had heard the rumours ashore had to be careful in their ships. Grumbling, muttering, talking in a way prejudicial to the good of the service was an offence. The older men picked their company carefully when they spoke of these things. The organisation of a ship, with Petty Officers and Chief Petty Officers living apart from the men in their own messes, made it easier for ratings to find quiet places to talk away from official ears. Some of them were members of benefit and welfare societies, such as the Royal and Ancient Order of Buffaloes, and the Buffaloes on *Rodney* discussed the rumours when they met in the ship's bandroom on the cruise North.

There were rumours in Chatham, too. Howard Morris was signal boy in the *Repulse*, a Chatham ship which also sailed on the 7th and he remembers discussion of the impending cuts by men involved in the welfare committees. 'Every sailor on the lower deck needed every penny he had. He had to count every penny. The longer they were in, the more they suffered, because the few pennies of badge money [the long-service good-conduct badges] were not much.'

Was there a leak? Secrets were certainly hard to keep in the Navy. A signal passed through a number of hands, and even coded signals seem to have formed the basis of rumours. Lower-deck intelligence came in the form of 'buzzes', rumours that passed from one friend to another – they were often remarkably accurate, but few men were prepared to take any action on the basis of a 'buzz'. In any case, the prospect of a universal application of the 1925 rates had been clearly spelt out in the May Report, and discussed in the sailors' newspaper the *Fleet*. By the time the Fleet arrived at Invergordon, on the afternoon of Friday 11 September, the rumour had grown in conviction but it was still of restricted circulation. Nevertheless, it had soured the atmosphere on many ships. A young midshipman from the *Warspite* went ashore on Friday evening with the ship's running team.

> There was a marked lack of enthusiasm among the sailors, an indication that something was wrong. 'This year,' I wrote, 'the officers form a group in front and the remainder straggle behind. Last year it was the reverse.' That evening one of the sailors in the running team confided in me that there was going to be trouble about pay cuts [H. Fox].

The weekend was a time to relax and recover from the mock-battle exercise. The arrival of the Fleet was a big event for the small town of Invergordon, and the annual Highland Games were always arranged to coincide with its coming. Many of the younger men and boys went ashore for the games on Saturday afternoon. Others went to take part in the Fleet football matches which were taking place. The town had few commercial entertainments, and many sailors preferred not to go ashore anyway as they could not afford to spend money, but Saturday's weather was fine and some went just to enjoy a stroll ashore. A few went in to the naval canteen, a long hut with a bar at one end which sold food, chocolate and cheap weak beer. Those who went in there found a group of men from the *Rodney* and the *Adventure* discussing the pay cuts worriedly.

The Admiralty Fleet Order was officially to go on ship's notice boards during this Saturday, and the full details of the cuts were to be in the Press on Sunday. Thus men were officially supposed to discover the cuts late on Saturday or early Sunday. In fact there were a number of slips in this procedure: although the Fleet Order appears to have been received by the Admirals on Saturday, the copies for general distribution did not reach the *Hood* until Tuesday 15th (Report of Proceedings).

Officers were supposed to be forewarned by an Admiralty Letter dispatched on the 10th, which the Atlantic Fleet ships were intended to pick up on arrival on Friday 11th. This letter was an outline of the policy decision to abolish the old rate of pay. As an explanation for the men it was quite useless, even dangerous; the text was provocative. It read, in part,

> The revised rates of pay introduced in 1925 for ratings and junior officers were the result of the report of the Committee on the Pay of State Servants in 1923, which expressed the opinions –
>
> (a) that none of the Fighting Services err on the side of paying officers of the highest rank too much;
> (b) that the pay of officers of middle rank is not excessive, subject to such adjustment on cost of living grounds as is already provided for in the regulations;
> (c) that the pay of junior officers is more than is necessary or even fair to the rest of the community, and
> (d) that the pay of the men is too high and should be reduced in correspondence with the wages paid in civil employment.
>
> In 1925, as you are aware, junior officers and men

already in the service were nevertheless allowed to retain the advantage of the existing higher rates of pay.
At the present time, however, when the need for reducing the national expenditure is urgent and the community as a whole is being called upon to make heavy
sacrifices, it is found to be impossible to permit this
concession to continue.

As a piece of explanation it was unlovely, but it should have
served at least to give Divisional Officers and their superiors
a few hours' notice of what would be in the Admiralty Fleet
Order. In the event, however, it was only received on Friday
by four men at Invergordon – Rear-Admirals French and
Astley-Rushton, Captain Bellairs in *Rodney* and Captain Dibben in *Adventure*. The two Admirals apparently did nothing
at all with their copies. The copy addressed to the
Commander-in-Chief, which was intended for general distribution by his staff, sat in a bundle of mails addressed to
his flagship *Nelson*. Since *Nelson* did not arrive until Sunday,
the bundle waited unopened (C. H. Herdman, *Naval Review*,
July 1976). The copy addressed personally to Tomkinson,
now in command of the Fleet, had been sent by mistake to
Renown, a ship he had left two months before.

Even if Tomkinson had received a copy of the letter for
himself, there is no particular reason to suppose that he
would have done anything with it. He would have assumed
– as he did assume when he finally discovered the existence
of the letter after *Nelson*'s arrival – that every ship in the
Fleet had its own copy. The real problem was that the distribution of the letter was a matter for the staff, and the staff
had been left behind in Portsmouth on board *Nelson*.

The only Captains to receive this letter on the Friday when
it was meant to be distributed were Captains Bellairs and
Dibben. Captain Bellairs addressed the crew of *Rodney* on
Friday, telling them of the impending cuts and urging them
to take any complaints to the proper channels. Dibben, in
Adventure, read his copy of the letter and apparently ordered

it to be placed on the ship's notice board. Men read it on Saturday morning, and began complaining to their Divisional Officers; a number went ashore from both ships in the afternoon with the specific intention of being able to grumble away from their officers' ears. Men from other ships joined them and listened, and many took what they were hearing as confirmation of the rumours they had already heard. Some had also seen the Saturday papers, which mentioned a reduction to the 1925 rates, but in a rather confused way, and others got the impression that everyone was going to suffer a 1s. cut, whether they were on the old rate of pay or not.

George Hill, the Commander's Writer in *Norfolk*, had not gone ashore. He had the exceptional privilege of using his own radio on board, and that was where he found his entertainment: most evenings he could be found at the radio with his friend Len Wincott, listening to dance music. On Friday, he had tuned in to the BBC news at six o'clock. After the news, he heard an item on reactions to the cuts and to a White Paper which made it clear that there was indeed to be a general reduction to the 1925 rates of pay.

George, having served on the Benevolent Trust, understood what this would mean. Most men retained the legal minimum of their pay – one day's pay a week – and allotted the rest to their families. If daily pay fell by 1s., the family income would go down by 6s. a week. Furniture would be re-possessed; some families would be evicted.

He told the Commander what he had heard, and also passed the news on to men in the mess-deck, and the boat's crew, who were ferrying men and mails. They passed the word around. When the nine o'clock news came, George was back listening to the radio, with Len Wincott.

> Len took it very quietly. Don't forget he was a single man; but I'm confident that his upbringing played a great part in what he did in the next few days. He had been born into abject misery and poverty. He was one

of eight children. His father was nothing more than a drunken sot, who earned for himself the name of Ivan the Terrible, because he used to thrash his children unmercifully, with a strap.

Each day, George Hill produced fifty copies of a news-sheet. The *Norfolk*'s news-sheet for Saturday carried the story that he had heard on the news, with Hill's additional comment, 'It is thought these cuts could carry serious repercussions.'

Sunday was the day when the first official news of the cuts began to circulate through the Fleet, as some ships received the Admiralty Fleet Order. While those officers who understood the real meaning of the cuts were outraged on behalf of the men under them, the men themselves found their worst fears confirmed. In many cases they had refused to believe the rumours until they had final confirmation; now there could be no doubt that the promises that had been made in the past were worthless.

> What I didn't call the Admiralty is nobody's business. My heart fell through. I was on four and six a day, and I had to get clothing for the children. My heart fell through. That was the general feeling of all of us.

Buck Donovan, stoker in the *Rodney*, expresses the universal feeling among the older men. He could not imagine how he was going to manage. Whatever the statistics said about prices having fallen, the truth was that in the naval towns rents had stayed high, and extra 'wealth' was more than absorbed by growing children. 'There was no discussion in my mess, but a mate of mine said "What the hell are we going to do now?" There were many suggestions, "We'll see the skipper," and such things.'

But it was obvious that the officers could do nothing to help; they had been kept completely in the dark. And the cuts were to come into force on 1 October, less than three weeks away. There would be no time to make any new arrangements for paying off hire purchase debts or repaying other debts: men with families would be unable to get home and sort things out before the cuts began.

'We were prepared to take a reasonable cut in a patriotic spirit. But the reaction of the men was just incredulous. It was bloody mad. The Admiralty had pulled a fast one.' That was the reaction of Robert Brown, who was serving as an Artificer in *York*. He held the rank, as a fully qualified artisan, of Chief Petty Officer: a rank which in theory should have carried an obligation to ensure that he did everything possible to encourage men to rely on their officers for help. But he, like many of this new class of Artificer Petty Officers, had little confidence in most commissioned officers at the best of times. Such confidence as had existed had now been removed completely. It was obvious to everyone that the officers were impotent. It was also obvious that something would have to be done to demonstrate to the Admiralty that the sailors could not and would not take this lying down. So far as the sailors were concerned the Admiralty, personified by the new First Lord, Austen Chamberlain, had revealed exactly what they thought of the lower-deck – absolutely nothing.

> Chamberlain – they'd have crucified him if they could have bloody got at him. He thought none of the Navy had any intelligence at all. To take a shilling a day from each person was bloody silly. It was contempt. They thought the chaps were unintelligent. Did they think we couldn't do arithmetic? A percentage cut would have been all right, but to cut everybody by a shilling – well, it just wasn't on. And the officers were losing three per cent! We were losing a quarter of our pay! [Sam Wheat, Leading Seaman, HMS *Hood*].

Most of those who did not see the Admiralty Fleet Order on Sunday morning learned of the cuts from the Sunday papers, which now carried full details. Sunday began with divine service and while Church of England services were held in each ship, the Nonconformists went to church ashore. It was the Nonconformists who brought back the papers, and in a number of ships the Sunday paper was pinned up on the notice board before the Fleet Order had been received.

Catholics and Wesleyans also assembled from the whole Fleet for their services – the Wesleyans in *Rodney*, the Catholics in *Malaya*. Since the *Malaya* was a newly commissioned ship, her crew did not know each other well enough to say what they felt even in the semi-privacy of their mess-deck.

> Everyone was eyeing one another, not knowing if you dare speak. You had to be careful who you spoke to – that chap having his dinner alongside me, if I say something, will he shop me? When you've only been together for a few days – well, it takes a long time for a ship's company to settle down [J. V. Hooper, Royal Marine, *Malaya*].

But it was in *Malaya* that the idea of some kind of meeting ashore seems to have been first mentioned. Wincott claims, and Hill supports the claim, that he asked *Norfolk*'s Catholics to sound out men from the other ships at their service, and tell him what the reaction was to the idea of a meeting in the canteen. Rumours began to spread that something would be happening there later in the afternoon.

Shore patrols were provided by different ships each day: this day it was the *Warspite*'s turn. At about midday *Warspite*'s Master-at-Arms reported the rumour of a meeting ashore, and it was passed on to Gunner Wood, the Patrol Officer.

At about the same time, Lieutenant-Commander Harry Pursey on the *Hood* was reporting to his Commander, McCrum, that there was a likelihood of mutiny in the fleet. He had been shown a Sunday paper by a trusted lower-deck man with the comment 'The men won't stand for it.' He warned McCrum that the time for trouble would be at 8a.m. on Tuesday morning, when *Hood*, *Valiant*, *Rodney* and *Nelson* would all be going to sea for exercises. McCrum responded

53

'Don't worry. We shall be all right on this ship!' (Pursey box 11).

Sunday was not a very exciting day in Invergordon: the town was shut down for the Sabbath. Half of each ship's company were allowed ashore, but since the only attraction open was the rather dismal canteen, few men usually took much notice of the opportunity unless they were footballers or hardened drinkers. But on this Sunday, the number of libertymen ran into many hundreds. Over a hundred went from *Rodney* alone, including Cyril Bond, who was known on board as a particularly outspoken and troublesome man. They also included a contingent of the bitterest men of all – those who had already served twelve years, and had just re-engaged for a further ten to collect a pension. In effect, they would now serve two-and-a-half of those ten years without pay. And pensions, too, had been cut.

Discussions over the canteen beer built up slowly. The canteen was exclusively for the lower ranks – Petty Officers had their own canteen – and they sat and talked as usual in groups of ship-mates. The emphasis on inter-ship competition normally developed a certain identification between men and their ships – though this was rather weaker in the Atlantic Fleet, where about a quarter of the men changed after each leave, than in other Fleets. At about six o'clock Harold Prestage, a Royal Naval Volunteer Reserve boy from the *Hood* who had been enjoying his first outing in a warship, wandered in to the canteen to buy some pigs' trotters and noticed nothing strange. But as the football matches ended men continued to join the groups talking, and a strange taunting began.

> They were saying about this money had been deducted from the seamen's pay, and they said, 'Now the *Valiant*'s crew has just arrived here and they are having nothing to do with it.' One of our chaps said, 'What do you mean?' They called us yellow. So we said, 'Well, there's a lot of our ship's company are JX ratings

[already on the new rate of pay], which it doesn't concern.' So they said, 'It will concern them later on.' So of course the *Valiant*'s crew said, 'We'll go in with you' [Charles Edwards, AB, *Valiant*].

A new form of co-operation was appearing in the Navy. Tommy Atkins, the ship's postman from *Malaya*, who was twenty-five years old, watched with fascination as the men talked and stirred each other into belligerence. He was half-horrified, as he knew what had happened in Chile: it had been a subject of discussion on board, because the *Almirante Latorre*, the ship that led the Chilean mutiny, had already been in Devonport for a refit and many men now in the *Malaya* had made friends on board her. They identified sympathetically with the Chilean sailors, who had been so brutally crushed when they protested over their own pay cuts.

> The Sunday meeting was the most important, because it started things off [he told me]. People started asserting themselves. Whereas they were timid before about what they were going to say, they started reasserting themselves and getting the gift of the gab, you might say. They were saying, 'What are we going to do?' 'Are we going to put up with this?' 'It's likely to turn our wives into prostitutes back home – what are we going to do about it? We've got to do something.' At least a couple of dozen of them was saying this and others was following and repeating what they were saying.

Towards seven o'clock things began to get really heated. Robert Fraser, who was serving the beer, remembers men clambering on the tables in different corners of the room and addressing the group nearest to them. Bond, in one corner, suggested that they should go to London to press their case on the Admiralty. When the question arose of how they should get there, it was proposed that they commandeer a train.

Few men took such notions seriously, but they were attempts to grapple with a real problem. There had been no official attempt to discuss these cuts with the men or their officers before they were introduced. It seemed impossible that if anyone understood their impact the cuts would be allowed to go through, but there was no constitutional way of explaining the impact of these cuts to the Admiralty. Neither the official welfare system nor the internal complaints procedure of the Navy could possibly be expected to yield the swift positive response that was needed before 1 October. Some kind of demonstration was the only answer.

It must have been about this time – around a quarter to seven – that Rear-Admiral Astley-Rushton walked past the canteen and noticed that a speech was being made. He must have had some suspicion that trouble was building up: the canteen was well away from the town. He hurried off to find the shore patrol, who were at the pier.

While he was doing this, Wincott had got onto a table and begun to address the whole assembly. There was clearly something remarkable about this man: he was a fluent and vigorous talker who was capable of talking clear good sense, but he also had presence. Harold Marris, a seaman on the *York* who had grown up with Wincott in Leicester, remembers him as the boyhood leader of whatever was going on – a born orator. Donovan, from the *Rodney*, clearly remembers the impact he made in that noisy canteen: 'He said, "Men, go aboard. It'll be passive resistance and no bloodshed." For a minute there was nothing said – then you couldn't stop men talking.'

Wincott's proposal was, as he later explained, for a strike 'like the miners'. It was absurd to think of leaving the ships and setting out for London. What they *could* do – and it was an idea which was already in the air, and which had already been mentioned by officers and men on a number of ships – was refuse to put to sea. 'Passive resistance', 'strike' – nobody used the word 'mutiny' then, and they still refuse to use it now.

There were good reasons for believing that such action was not, in fact, a mutiny. Quite apart from the fact that the word seems to suggest a violent attack on the officers and the seizure of a ship, men were well aware that the Navy itself had distinguished between this kind of action and 'mutiny' earlier in the year.

On 4 January there had been trouble on board the submarine depot ship *Lucia* in Devonport. The ship was due to join the rest of the Atlantic Fleet for the spring cruise the next day, and men were looking forward to going ashore for the last time to say goodbye to their families before setting out for Gibraltar. It was a Sunday. Without notice, all leave was cancelled: the ship was filthy after taking on coal, and it had to be painted before going to sea. A Leading Seaman persuaded the hands to go on strike. When the Master-at-Arms ordered them to fall in, they refused and closed the hatch, sealing themselves in their mess-deck.

The seamen were taken off under armed guard, and sailing was cancelled, but the Commander-in-Chief, Plymouth, issued a statement to the Press that said, 'It can be said at once that the use of the word mutiny would be unjustifiable.' Four men were Court Martialled, but they were not charged with mutiny. Had they been – and there seems little doubt that they could have been accused of 'mutiny not accompanied by violence' – the ringleaders would have been liable to the death penalty. Instead they were charged with *wilful disobedience of a lawful command*, which was punishable by imprisonment and, at worst, dismissal with disgrace from the service.

There was thus a strong belief in the Atlantic Fleet that strike action was not considered mutiny.

Wincott's proposal had caught the mood of the men, but they were going to have to be very sure of the solidarity of the whole Fleet before they could seriously consider an act of mass indiscipline. Wincott says he took down the names of men who agreed to sound out opinion on each ship and report back the next evening. The American Vice-Consul in

Southampton was told by a Petty Officer from *Nelson* that a spokesman was indeed selected from each ship (letter of F. Willard Calder, 20 Sept., US Nat. Arch. 841.30/95). It was certainly the case that everyone believed another meeting was needed on Monday, when the other watch would have their time ashore.

Gunner Wood took his patrol to the canteen, and found that the situation was becoming rowdy, with glasses being thrown about and some windows being broken. He signalled for reinforcements from the *Warspite*, and went to find the pier patrol.

Richard Tyler was the Commander's Writer in *Warspite*, and when the call for reinforcements was received he was summoned by Commander Fallowfield. Tyler was himself one of the men hardest hit by the cuts – he had just signed on for his second term of service.

> The Commander said that he wanted twelve marines and so many seamen ready on the quarter-deck in twenty minutes to land ashore with him. My job was to inform the Sergeant-Major in charge of marines, which I did, and then I got twelve names off the list and told our messenger to find these chaps and tell them to get gaiters on, and a belt and stick, and get up on the quarter-deck at once. Well, the messenger came back and I said, 'How have you got on?' He said, 'Well, I haven't found one. If I go to a chap and say, "Are you so-and-so?", he says, "No, I'm not." ' We'd only been together for a few days, so we didn't know who was who. So we sounded off on the bugle, duty watch to fall in – that's the whole bunch. So they fell in, because they didn't know what it was for. Then when they fell in, the Commander went along and said, 'Right, 2–4–6–8–10–12. You others I don't want.' They went ashore with our Commander.

The mood of the Fleet was not only sullen, it was infecting the marines as well as the seamen. The reinforcing patrol included, besides seamen, marines and the Commander, a Lieutenant, a Petty Officer and a marine NCO.

Meanwhile Gunner Wood had gone back to the canteen to try to restore order. He saw men from *Norfolk*, *Rodney* and *Warspite*, among others, making speeches on a table, but by the time the reinforcements arrived it was all over.

While this was going on, the *Nelson* was finally arriving at Cromarty Firth. She had had a dismal journey; men knew of the pay cuts from a scoop in the Portsmouth *Evening News* before setting out on the Friday, and they were profoundly depressed.

> It was very difficult to discuss the cuts, but you could see the disheartened looks on the men's faces, especially the married ones. It was a very disheartening thing to see some of the old timers and the way they suffered [Reginald Smither, 19-year-old seamen in *Nelson*].

> We knew there was going to be cuts, like, but we didn't know they was going to do a silly thing like that. A shilling a day off every man! Well, married men, it hit them hard.

> There was meetings in the smoking room, up forrard, on the way North. When you got up there it was like a pea-soup atmosphere, you could hardly see your-selves. Meetings were going on more or less contin-ually. The main speaker there was an old three-badge torpedoman who had taken on for his second term. He was saying it was ridiculous [R. Harbin, Stoker 1st Class, *Nelson*].

As the crew of the *Nelson* stood on the upper deck of their ship, giving the traditional silent salute to the vessels they passed on their way to anchor, they were astonished to hear cheering coming from the other ships. As soon as they anchored, and boats began to pass between the *Nelson* and other ships, slips of paper began to come aboard telling the *Nelson*'s crew what was going on. The Fleet was in a ferment. That night there were meetings aboard every ship, as men passed the word around of what had happened and what was to happen.

Considering the excitement – which had brought men back to their ships loudly singing 'The More We Are Together' – the senior command of the Fleet seem to have remained astonishingly blind. Astley-Rushton noted later that he reported the canteen speech-making to Tomkinson, on board the *Hood*, as soon as he had summoned the patrol, but for some reason there is no record of his visit in the *Hood*'s log. The Captain of the *Warspite* interviewed the three men from his ship identified in the canteen, and was given a clear indication of what was afoot – one of them, Bousefield, stressed the need for 'passive resistance'. Tomkinson had also sent his Chief Staff Officer to watch the canteen meeting (Report of Proceedings). Yet when he heard the reports of the Staff Officer and the Commander of the *Warspite* that night, he decided that it had no significance for the discipline of the Fleet. At half-past ten that night, Rear-Admiral French came over from the *Warspite* to consult with Tomkinson, at French's own request. There are copies of the signals in Commander Pursey's extensive collection of Invergordon material. But neither French nor Tomkinson ever mentioned this meeting, in any of their later reports and post-mortems of events.

Commander Pursey's papers also contain a letter from a Chief Petty Officer on the *Hood* who had witnessed the canteen meeting. 'On return aboard I asked to see my Senior Divisional Officer. . .I told him what I thought was under way and he said, "Get below or you're in the Commander's report for prosecution in the morning." '

If the men were going to mount some kind of protest, nobody wanted to know. Perhaps it was simply that no one believed that anything could happen – that all the talk was as wild as that of the men returning to the *Warspite*, who were talking of going over to Lossiemouth and burning Ramsay MacDonald's house there. But perhaps there was more to it than that. There were officers – some very senior officers – who also felt that the Admiralty had betrayed the Navy, broken the contracts of the men and reneged on its promises. Officers who felt that the Admiralty had failed the Navy over and over again in the years of harsh economy, and who felt as impotent to protest as the men on the lower-deck. Tomkinson received his personal demonstration of the Admiralty's care for the Navy that evening, when the Chief of Staff, Rear-Admiral Colvin, newly arrived in *Nelson*, came to visit him. Colvin told him of the Admiralty Letter about the cuts, assuming that Tomkinson had received a personal copy. Tomkinson had never even heard of it.

His own copy arrived in the middle of the next morning. It had been addressed to him in a ship which he had left two months earlier. He began drafting a letter of protest at this incompetence.

At about the same time on Monday morning, he signalled to the Admiralty.

> *Important*. There was a slight disturbance in the Royal Naval canteen at Invergordon yesterday Sunday evening caused by one or two ratings endeavouring to address those present on the subject of reduction in pay. I attach no importance to the incident from a general disciplinary point of view but it is possible it may be reported in an exaggerated form by the press. Matter is still being investigated.

He was later to write that a significant cause of the trouble to follow was the belief that normal channels of complaint 'were in this case valueless, and that the men had no other course than the one they took. . .It is difficult to avoid the conclusion that there is foundation for such a feeling among the men' (ADM 178/110 no. 6 RPI).

5
Preparing Action

Before the disciplined man can throw off authority, he
has to be worked up into an abnormal condition.

Lieutenant-Commander C. Drage,
'Some Modern Naval Mutinies', Conclusion

If Tomkinson was going to report the canteen incident at all,
why should he wait until the middle of the following morning before getting around to it?

The likeliest answer seems to be that he and everyone else
took it much more seriously than that telegram suggests.
The *Malaya* and the *Warspite* were due to go to sea on Monday morning, and it seems likely that Tomkinson wanted to
see whether they would get safely away before deciding
what to tell the Admiralty. Once they got under way without
trouble there was some euphoria amongst officers in the
Hood that the rumoured stoppage of work had not taken
place (Pursey/16).

If anyone was comparing these two ships with the rest of
the Fleet, they were making a serious mistake: they were
both newly commissioned ships whose crews did not know
each other well enough to trust each other. The only similar
ship was *Repulse*. Their crews contented themselves with
angry muttering. As the *Malaya* reached Lossiemouth, there
was talk among the men of turning her guns on Ramsay
MacDonald's house there.

If that had happened, Ramsay MacDonald might not have
been too surprised. He had an unnerving experience over
the weekend on board the aircraft carrier *Courageous*, which

would have convinced anyone that the sailors were not too enthusiastic about their pay cuts. He had gone onto the *Courageous* on Saturday, to watch the Schneider Trophy air race. It was an event which attracted great public attention, and Britain had a revolutionary aircraft in the race, Mitchell's Supermarine S6B. Saturday was an unfortunate day for this, as it was the day when the Admiralty Fleet Order listing the pay cuts was issued. Len Johnson, a stoker, claims to have a clear recollection of the Prime Minister's visit.

> The skipper cleared lower deck. The whole crew was assembled in the hangar. All planes were put up on the flight decks, giving us space. When we'd all assembled inside the hangar the Captain introduced Ramsay Mac-Donald and his retinue, who stood on a dais. Ramsay MacDonald spoke to us, then the Captain, in the usual tradition, called for three hearty cheers for Ramsay Mac-Donald. We were all so darned incensed that we'd have blown Ramsay MacDonald through a torpedo tube.
>
> So the Captain gets his hat in the traditional way, waves it round, 'Hip! Hip! Hip!. . .' They all of them went R-R-R-R-P! One bloody great raspberry!
>
> Of course the Captain's face was as red as a beetroot, so was Ramsay's and everybody else. So he had another go. Round again. 'Hip! Hip! Hip!. . .' 'R-R-R-R-P!' Again. Because you always give three anyway. Round he goes again, and he got the biggest result of all time. . .

At this point my skills in transliteration fail; I cannot adequately convey the vigour with which an old sailor can illustrate a thousand men blowing the biggest raspberry in the world.

Every story improves in the telling, and most of the stories I have been told have had fifty years to mature: perhaps they sometimes express the spirit of a moment, rather than its external form. But the image of a Captain hopelessly and mechanically locked in the stylised response of three cheers, thank God no more but oh God! no less. . .

Ramsay MacDonald got the message. The race was postponed because of bad weather; it was flown on Sunday instead. The British plane won. But the Prime Minister did not see the triumph after all. He had retreated to Chequers.

The *Malaya*'s crew spared MacDonald's house, and in the cold light of a new day those of them who had been at Sunday's canteen discussion doubted if anything more would happen. Tyler, in the *Warspite*, was convinced that the men left in Cromarty Firth would not be allowed to go ahead with their plan to hold a further meeting in the canteen: there had been talk in *Warspite* too of burning MacDonald's house, and he was convinced that shore leave would be cancelled in the Fleet at anchor on Monday.

There was no shortage of indications that further discussions ashore would lead to trouble. On Monday morning the Captain of the *Nelson* addressed his crew on the subject of the cuts: when he told them that the ship would be sailing on exercise next morning, the torpedoman who had been agitating against the cuts corrected him: 'No it won't sir!'(Harbin).

Captain Cochrane, in the *Repulse*, addressed his ship's company when he discovered that shore leave was not to be cancelled: he warned them that they should stay away from shore meetings. Since the *Repulse* was a long way from Invergordon, it was reasonable to discourage the men from landing there, and the shorter trip to Cromarty was recommended instead.

In the *York*, Captain Custance attempted to reconcile his men to their new rates of pay by reading from the Admiralty Letter. This was in accordance with an instruction sent by Tomkinson that morning – Tomkinson having only discovered the existence of the letter the night before. It was not a document well suited to the mood of the moment; indeed the Captain of *Valiant* considered it best to ignore this order (Drage papers).

The letter did not go down well in the *York*.

> It was greeted with gasps of astonishment by everyone, particularly the married men who would be hit the hardest.
>
> After reading the instruction the Captain added 'I'm sorry about this but if you find you can't manage your wife can be asked to take in washing to augment your pay.'
>
> A very angry voice from the rear ranks shouted, 'You fat bastard! How would you like your old woman to crash out the dirties?' Whereupon the Captain immediately ordered the quarterdeck to be cleared and the ship's company resumed their normal duties amid much discussion and dissension [Letter from W. W. Knight].

There was plainly nervousness throughout the Fleet at officer level. Pursey, the Mate of the Upper Deck of the *Hood*, warned his Commander that they should take care during the day's drill not to disturb anything which could become a problem if the men stopped work. The Commander was diffident about asking the men to do any work at all: 'We are only going to do a little General Drill this morning,' he told them.

There were other indications, too. During the morning break large numbers of men gathered on the forecastles of many ships, and the return to work was hesitant, especially in *Rodney*. It was as though the crews were watching each other to see if anyone wanted to take a lead in initiating some protest action. The drills were carried out without enthusiasm, and some men packed in early (Pursey papers, box 21).

Given all these indications of real trouble brewing, why was shore leave not cancelled for the coming afternoon? Despite Tomkinson's bland signal about Sunday night's unrest ashore, Naval Intelligence had been sufficiently concerned to dispatch at least one undercover agent, Sam

Bassett, to 'assist the local police and security agents' (S. Bassett, *Royal Marine*, 1962). Bassett's account, which was evidently written many years later from memory, says that he was told to go on Monday and arrived on Tuesday in the early evening. It is curious that there is no mention of this in the Admiralty papers. One may perhaps deduce that Naval Intelligence kept their information separate for much of the time. They were probably acting on the basis of their own intelligence reports; Bassett was asked to compare his mission with 'going behind the lines in enemy territory', which suggests that they had heard something alarming.

It was certainly known in the *Hood*, both from the reports received and from the interrogation of some of the *Hood*'s own crew who had been in the canteen, that another meeting was likely and that some form of strong action was being called for. It is also clear that many men expected leave to be stopped. There was a buzz in the Fleet that it had been.

Many kinds of explanation have been offered for leave not being cancelled. It has been said that senior officers were quite out of touch with the men, that where promotion was so hard to come by, everyone was afraid of making themselves conspicuous by reporting anything they did know – but in the light of all the very plain evidence being shouted aloud, one might think that it would take deliberate deafness not to hear, deliberate blindness not to see. It has been suggested that cancelling leave might have precipitated trouble by aggravating the men unnecessarily – but *Warspite* and *Malaya* had already sailed without any repercussions in the rest of the Fleet, and thus an immediate dispersal of the Fleet might have been successful. Going ashore at Invergordon was no great treat. Under normal circumstances, few men would bother to go ashore there on a Monday. Their only purpose in going in any numbers would be to discuss the pay cuts.

It is true that dispersing the Fleet would be decisive action of a kind that Tomkinson might not feel strong enough to take. His whole life had been spent as a second-in-command, he lacked visible attributes of positive leadership, his authority over his staff and junior admirals was weak. But it is action which one might have expected would receive strong backing from Astley-Rushton, who certainly was capable of taking decisions when he needed to.

Another suggestion has been that there was a feeling that men should be allowed to blow off steam, and that a discussion ashore could not possibly lead to mutiny; the very idea of mutiny was unthinkable to officers, which is why the warnings being given were treated so lightly. That is an explanation which would carry more conviction if there had not been a number of well-known acts of indiscipline in the recent past, most lately the *Lucia* affair.

There was a feeling among the men that they had an unusual license on Monday afternoon. Leave was allowed early in the afternoon for footballers, later for everyone else. Since leave was given to alternate watches, those who had been ashore on Sunday were not entitled to go again on Monday, but there was a custom of ignoring the rule if a man could find a substitute to stay aboard in his place, and this was used to the full. George Hill, the Commander's Writer in *Norfolk*, willingly agreed to act as Wincott's substitute. Before going ashore, Wincott addressed a meeting on the forecastle, telling them what was being planned. The number of men who went ashore was quite extraordinary for a Monday at Invergordon – more went from the *Rodney*, for example, than had gone ashore on Saturday or Sunday, when there had been a fine weekend and entertainments ashore.

Harry Marris was in the *York*'s football team, which was playing a final in one of the many competitions run in the Fleet. About half an hour before the match ended he saw his old childhood acquaintance, Len Wincott, calling to him from the touchline. Wincott was with a group of men going up to the canteen, and Marris was asked to come as soon as he could make it. Wincott carried on to the canteen, and arrived to find discussion in full flow. At first it had been animated but disorganised, with men grouped round tables talking vigorously, but as the numbers increased, tables were cleared away to make standing room.

William Symons, from the *Nelson*, had not bothered with the football, and had gone straight to the canteen.

> There wasn't much went on. It was just a general meeting. There were several spokesmen on the platform. All Chiefs and Petty Officers were shut out. Beer was served, but not once the meeting was on. We were all drinking beer when the canteen was opened, and directly the meeting started the doors were closed, no beer served, and we just sat and drunk up our pints and listened to whoever was speaking. They talked mostly about the Government, about Ramsay MacDonald and Snowden and also how the twenty-five per cent cut would hurt the lower-paid man in the Navy, those on the flat rate of four bob a day, and the hardships that it would incur – it was us that was getting the hardship. Different spokesmen got up from different ships. The only people that knew what they were going to talk about were these ringleaders; the decision to strike was taken there, that night. We knew we were going to do something, but not actually what until it was decided in the canteen.

A man from the *Valiant* takes up the story:

> We decided to – well, more or less down tools, go on strike, that's what we called it. The spokesmen said that we ought to show our disapproval of what was going to happen and the only way to show that disapproval was to just stop work. They stood up. . .I think there was two or three men spoke. I can't say who they were because they were from other ships. There was nobody from our ship. People had removed their cap ribbons, so we're not supposed to know. . .there was so many of us we could hardly move. We had a show of hands,

what we should do, and it was agreed that we should down tools.

Then we heard a banging at the door. Someone looked out the window and said, 'It's the Officer of the Patrol.' We'd got the door on a latch so that he couldn't push in if he wanted to.

The Officer of the Patrol was Robert Elkins. He had been told by his Captain that this meeting was likely, and he had left six men in the vicinity of the canteen to keep an eye on things. He had now received a message that they were locked out, and had come to find out what was happening.

He was allowed in, with a certain amount of barracking, and said that he wanted to hear what was going on.

> We said – or the people at the door said – you can come in, but the Patrol stays outside. So the officer was given safe conduct right to the spokesman. He was told that he would not be molested, but he said that he wanted to hear what was going on. But he was too late, because we'd already made the plans what we wanted to make. The only thing he heard was the winding up of the meeting. (Anonymous AB, HMS *Valiant*)

Elkins then noticed two civilians near the door, and went to discover what they were doing there. As he was speaking to them a glass was thrown and shattered over his head. There was hostility towards the man who did this – he was later thumped for it – but there was plainly a danger that if Elkins stayed things might turn nasty. The men around him linked arms and walked firmly towards the door, propelling him out. At this point, Marris arrived from his football match.

> As I got to the door of the canteen the officer was just being breasted out of the building, and Wincott and two more men were standing on the counter speaking and arranging for what should be done. The officer said,

'Oh well, that's me, I've done all I can do.' And he was quite pleased about it, too, believe me.

People in there were mostly standing. The place was full. It wasn't chaos, nothing like that. It must have been arranged by somebody beforehand. They stressed that it was an injustice to take a shilling a day from an AB and a different percentage from higher ratings, and it was really unjust. I wouldn't say there was enthusiasm for taking action; it was sort of, 'Oh, we're resigned to it now.' Wincott was making concrete proposals about what should be done when various orders were given out for going to sea, that we should disobey these orders and all ships would do the same and acknowledge it by cheering to each other. Also I believe he said we'd heard from other ships via the wireless operators that we were being backed up, and one in particular was in the Mediterranean. They put it that we'd got backing, anyway.

No one from the *York* took part in the speaking. There was a show of hands – well, as far as I can remember they just said, 'All right, everybody OK?' and all the hands went up. There was no for and against, or anything like that.

The precise role played by Leonard Wincott has never been fully sorted out; he himself now denies that he spoke at all on the Monday, though he claims the credit for calling the Sunday's meeting and organising Monday's. Bassett, the Intelligence Officer, says that the canteen manager gave him an account of being shut out of the canteen and of listening from outside to a long speech by Wincott, but there seems to be a confusion in his writing between the Sunday and Monday evenings, and it is possible that he was influenced by Wincott's pamphlet published later in 1931. Robert Fraser, who was working behind the bar, says that the meeting never rose above incoherence at any time. In fact very few concrete decisions were made in the canteen for the

Fleet as a whole: the meeting was more of an expression of a popular will to back each other up in preventing the Fleet from going on exercises. The only men who seem to have gone in for detailed planning were a group from the *Nelson*. Coming from a ship where everyone was well used to pulling together, and conscious of their responsibility as the flagship of the Fleet, they sat down and worked out who would work and who would not, so that the ship would continue to function as a satisfactory place to live during the strike.

Elkins, meanwhile, had signalled for a reinforcing patrol and checked that the civilians were apparently harmless. Men began streaming away from the canteen, and as they did so some took the opportunity of apologising to him for the incident with the glass. A three-badge gunner from *Rodney* told him, 'We're doing this for you as well as for ourselves.'

Elkins followed a group of men who had gone down to a recreation field, and watched more speeches being made. Among the men speaking was Fred Copeman of the *Norfolk*, who was persuaded to climb on to the pavilion roof; he too spoke in favour of downing tools, but urged that it would be necessary to get this decision agreed by the men on each ship that night. A certain amount of taunting had been going on all the time, as one ship's company accused another of being 'yellow' and lacking the guts to take any action, and this continued. It took a long time, and a lot of talking and competitive barracking, for these men to work themselves up to a pitch where they would act. When they did, it would be on the basis that they could not let down other men on other ships. Loyalty to the Navy and their ships was being reforged into a solidarity of the lower-deck.

As the evening went on, men began to return to the canteen. Meanwhile the reinforcing patrol had landed, and discovered that conditions ashore indicated that men felt they had been released from the leash of naval discipline. The patrol was led by Lieutenant-Commander Robinson from the *Hood*, and he found that the normal respect given to a patrol was utterly lacking.

> On the way through the town we encountered a large number of Naval Ratings. . .the large majority of them failed to salute me or to pay any mark of respect, and ribald remarks were often made at the patrol. I considered it of primary importance to get to the canteen quickly and paid no attention. . .
>
> With Lieutenants Elkins and Pack-Beresford I went into the canteen by a side door which led behind the bar. No attention was paid to us and for some minutes I remained there and listened. The Canteen was very full – perhaps three hundred men – and many of them drunk. . .'Are we going to take our pay cuts lying down?' 'Shall the Fleet go to sea tomorrow? No!' 'It's no use going to the Captain,' etc. I blew a whistle for silence and stood up on the bar to talk to the men. For some minutes I was shouted down, but the majority of the men were shouting 'Give him a fair hearing' – 'Let's hear what he's got to say,' and eventually I had silence.
>
> I told the men they were going the wrong way about things and would only bring discredit on themselves and the Navy. That they should bring up any complaints in the service manner and that I would permit of no more speeches. This had the desired effect with the exception of one man who started a speech again. I obtained his name, and as by this time it was eight o'clock I closed the bar and closed the canteen [Report of Lieutenant-Commander Robinson, copy in Pursey Papers].

By now the structure of authority had disintegrated; the invisible restraints which bound men to obedience to their officers had been reworked by a frenzy of talk so that they were bound instead to support each other. Little beer had been drunk, but the air was charged with a nervous euphoria which was easily mistaken for drunkenness. Alfred

Williams was waiting on the jetty as the men came down to return to their ships. He was waiting to go aboard the tug *St Cyrus*, which was due to tow the target for the morning's firing practice. He was very young – only seventeen – but he had been brought up in a naval family, and had been in the Navy since he was eleven. He knew what to expect from a pack of drunken sailors, but this was different.

> It was quite frightening as a youngster to listen to all the shouting what was going on. There must have been several hundred men along the jetty, coming down, getting in the liberty boats. Some of them were quite inebriated to say the least, but on the whole not too bad. They were shouting 'Don't forget, *Rodney!*' 'OK, *Nelson.*' Up in Invergordon they had been singing the 'Red Flag' – I had heard them. They weren't singing it because they were Communist, but because that's the way they felt at the time. They were feeling browned-off and more than browned-off, really disturbed about what was going to happen to their families.

The liberty boats left the jetty in an atmosphere of extraordinary confusion, with men still calling out to reinforce these new bonds of solidarity – 'Don't forget. Six o'clock tomorrow.' Six o'clock was the time when the day began on board ship. When men got back on to their ships, a frenzy of activity began.

Elkins had heard the men on the *Hood's* forecastle when he was on the pier: eventually he went aboard the *Hood* to report to Tomkinson. He was told that there had been trouble on board, and when he went to the wardroom he was invited to dinner next week 'if there was still a Navy'. The Captain and Commander of *Hood*, knowing that the shore meeting was likely to take place, had themselves been ashore in plain clothes to watch what happened. Now the Captain was at a dinner party, hosted by Tomkinson, for all the Captains and Admirals in Cromarty Firth. Elkins was summoned to their table to tell what had happened ashore.

In his own journal, he records that 'My impression was that they knew a great deal about it already and that it was not so bad as it sounded.'

It is possible, perhaps, to believe that leave was permitted on Monday because senior officers did not understand what was happening. It is not possible to believe that they were still so naive by Monday night. The idea that the whole Fleet might mutiny was probably too far-fetched to be taken seriously, but the probability of strike action in *Valiant* must have seemed credible to anyone who knew the ship, and it was highly probable that if *Valiant* did not go to sea on Tuesday morning, *Nelson* and *Rodney*, the next ships due out, would be in difficulties.

All three ships were battleships, under the command of Rear-Admiral French, who was at sea in *Warspite*. One of the curiosities of the next few hours is that no one seems to have made any signal to tell French what was going on.

Drage, in *Valiant*, certainly knew on Monday night that the men would refuse to take that ship to sea. 'I knew it was inevitable. I didn't see what else the men could do' (interview). Elkins's journal records what was being said in the *Valiant*'s wardroom on Tuesday:

> Astonishment was. . .expressed that a movement of such magnitude should have been allowed to take a hold without more being known about it or steps being taken to stop it. . .the final conclusion that was reached was that either the whole fleet had been taken unawares or that the senior officers were deliberately adopting what appeared to be a weak policy for political reasons [ELK/2, p. 4].

Tomkinson had the Captains of the whole Fleet in company at his dinner table. If there was going to be trouble – and the noises of the sailors coming back, combined with the reports coming in over dinner, made it plain that there was – communication with them might become difficult. At this moment, however, without the slightest difficulty, he could make whatever decision he wanted. He could order the Fleet to disperse by night. He could cancel the exercises. He could announce that for any of a dozen reasons there would be no sailing, and couple that with a statement that he was going to London to explain the hardship caused by the pay cuts. He decided to do nothing.

There was certainly a strong feeling at every level in the Fleet that the Admiralty had let them down very badly, and that the men's feeling that the officers were powerless was entirely justified. The new First Lord, Austen Chamberlain, was a man who had no following in the Navy, and the Sea Lords were, with the possible exception of Backhouse, regarded as either 'past it' (Field) or very weak and inadequate (Fuller and Preston). There was a universal feeling that the Navy had been kicked around for too long, that the Admiralty was dominated by civil servants who cared nothing for ships or the men in them and who were always willing to knuckle under to political pressure, whether it was for yet more economies or in matters of discipline. The significance of the cuts to a sailor's domestic budget was probably not appreciated by many senior officers yet, but there was a strong sense of injustice: the Admiralty had broken faith with the men on the old scale of pay, and betrayed the officers by not warning them.

When Admiral John Kelly later carried out an investigation into the events at Invergordon, he wrote to the First Sea Lord, 'The bitterness of adverse opinion and its entire unanimity against the Admiralty has astonished me. It transcends anything I have ever known.'

It seems impossible to ignore the possibility that there were very senior officers in the Fleet who were prepared to countenance the possibility that *Valiant*, possibly even *Nelson* and *Rodney*, would refuse to obey orders to sail, and that the Admiralty would have to respond by reconsidering the cuts. If that did happen, there was every reason to suppose that it would all be over very quickly and that the rest of the world would never get to hear of it.

Tomkinson's dinner party broke up sooner than sched-
uled, and the various Captains returned to their own ships.
When everything was over, they wrote reports of proceedings in their ships; there is a startling contrast between some
of their descriptions of Monday night and what was actually
taking place.

Captain Custance, of the *York*, says that on his return to
his ship he warned all officers that there was a serious
situation in the Fleet and reported to Tomkinson that everything on board was normal. In fact, men just back from the
canteen were going around the ship giving out instructions
on who was to strike and who was not. 'They was coming
around saying, "You're excused, you're excused" – that
would have been arranged earlier, in the canteen' (Marris).

One of the self-appointed strike leaders, a stoker by the
name of Eric Clegg, had fallen in while coming aboard, and
Commander Coppinger had dived in fully clothed to rescue
him. This had undoubtedly strengthened the affection of
the crew for their Commander, but it did not undermine the
will to strike.

The Captain of *Adventure* also claims that he found that
all was normal when he returned on board; can he really
have been totally ignorant of what was going on?

> There was singing and shouting in the liberty boat – we
> could hear it as they came alongside. What happened
> then – first of all they closed the portholes, screwed
> down the portholes, then they shut the two watertight
> doors, that was the one leading to the fo'c's'le and the
> one going out from the fo'c's'le, and then they were
> talking about striking, and they gave instructions. Now
> the instructions were, to the young people they said,
> 'We won't fall in. If an officer or a petty officer comes
> to you and gives you a direct order, and mentions your
> name, you would immediately go and do it.' But there
> were very few orders actually given to individuals. Very
> few and far between. Our instruction was to do nothing

but obey an individual order with your name [H. Ackland].

A situation like this was a great shock to many of the younger men on board; they had not been involved in the discussion up to now, since their pay was not affected and they did not have families to look after, so they were taken by surprise by the decisions that had been taken. Even more astonished were the small number of RNVR 'weekend sailors' on some of the ships, such as Douglas Stone in *Norfolk*. He was on his first fortnight of sea training, and had been impressed by the rigidity of discipline on board: when a Sub-Lieutenant had shouted 'Seaboats crew away' instead of 'Lifeboats crew away' in a minor emergency on the way to Invergordon, he had been charged with 'an act prejudicial to good order and discipline'. Stone's hammock was slung in the *Norfolk*'s recreation space, under the forecastle, and he had just settled down for the night on Monday when a mob of men surged in.

> We wondered what the deuce was going on especially when deadlights were put over the portholes and a massive matelot said, 'What are we going to do about these fucking rookies?' and he pointed at us. Others yelled, 'Chuck 'em out!' Another, a more commanding figure, said to us 'Can you keep your mouths shut?' and we nervously and speedily assured him we could. 'Well sit there and don't say a word!' he said.
>
> What followed was a series of serious, well-delivered speeches in which the speakers told of the misery and suffering and poverty that would be brought to their wives and children by the government's proposed cuts in pay. I was most impressed by these genuine expressions of opinion. It was eventually reported that the stokers in every ship had agreed not to get up steam the next morning and that everyone would refuse to obey orders.
>
> 'Mutiny, Mr Christian.' I could hardly believe my own

ears and a little shiver of apprehension set off a train of thought that encompassed officers shooting from the quarter deck.

Whatever role Wincott played in the canteen, there can be no doubt of his significance in organising the men in *Norfolk*, where he already had a considerable reputation.

> People yakked about him, you know, we talked about him on the gun deck. He seemed to have a big mouth, he did a lot of talking' [W. P. Wood].

According to Charles Boulton, who was on watch, it was Wincott who summoned the meeting in *Norfolk*'s recreation space.

> The Master-at-Arms and the Regulating Petty Officer never went near them. Nobody went near them. The bugle went at ten o'clock for 'Out Lights', but nobody tried to get in there. It went on until quarter past twelve. At quarter past twelve, when I went up to the recreation space hatch, they'd just opened the doors and you'd swear blind they'd dropped a smoke-bomb in, there were so many in there smoking.

The Master-at-Arms evidently had some idea of what was being said in there, for he reported that if the *Rodney* did not proceed to sea in the morning, the men planned to do no work in *Norfolk*. At eleven o'clock the Captain of *Norfolk* went to see the Rear-Admiral in charge of the cruiser squadron, Astley-Rushton, in *Dorsetshire*, where similar discussions were taking place.

The first ship due out in the morning was *Repulse*, where there was a large meeting on the forecastle, but it was *Valiant* that was likely to be the flash-point – the first ship due to leave the main anchorage. Here too there was a meeting on the forecastle, with men being told that they were all expected to strike from six o'clock next morning. It was a mass, crowd decision in *Valiant*: this was a ship which had never really settled down, and no natural leadership had emerged among the crew. There were individuals who were to make themselves prominent, but there was none of the sense of organisation which already existed among the mutineers in *York*, *Norfolk* and *Nelson*, the Fleet flagship.

It was impossible for the Captain of *Valiant* to be unaware of what was going on. He had come back from *Hood* with Elkins, and they had seen the men on *Rodney* cheering and signalling. Once aboard, Captain Scott summoned his Commander, Engineering Commander and Captain of Marines, and warned them to expect trouble. 'The Captain of Marines asked permission to parade the Marines armed at 06.00. This was refused' (Report of Proceedings).

Nelson's meeting was in the recreation space, and here clear distinctions were made between those men who were to work in the morning and those who were not. There was no need for ringleaders or spokesmen in *Nelson*; it was an efficient ship with a clear pattern of authority at every level, and the ship was quite capable of running itself without the intervention of officers.

> A handful of lower-deck lawyers handled the whole situation. We had no option but to trust them. I mean young seamen couldn't go to a Leading Seaman and say, 'You're wrong. You shouldn't have said that.' That's more than you dared do. Otherwise he would have clipped you round the ear and that was it. Where do you cry to? The only thing you could do was to put your fist up and have a go at him, but I never saw any of that [R. Smither].

Although the Commander-in-Chief was not aboard, *Nelson* still carried the Fleet's staff officers, and they can hardly have been ignorant of what was going on. Charles Williams was on the staff of Rear-Admiral Colvin, the Fleet's Chief of Staff.

> The men were very angry. I was talking to one of the

engine-room staff coming back from the canteen and he said 'If we don't get something done about it we're going to commandeer a train, we're going to go down to London ourselves.' I said, 'How are you going to go down to London from here?' He said 'We're going to commandeer a train.' I said, 'Well, how are you going to drive it?' He said, 'We've got artificers here, qualified engineers.' That was the mood at the time.

The *Rodney* was physically identical to the *Nelson*, but the state of morale on board was very different, more like that of *Valiant*. Men felt the need to whip themselves up to mass action. Tommy Hiscox, who was just a boy, was aware that meetings had been going on in the recreation room but was warned to stay away. 'There's lots going on, lots you shouldn't know about. You keep yourself out of trouble. I'll tell you when anything happens,' he was told by a stoker. On Monday night he lay awake feeling the atmosphere grow increasingly tense on board, until around midnight something broke. Then the stokers came to the boys' mess-deck and told them not to get up when called in the morning. If anyone insisted they get up, they were to tell him to look in the seamen's mess, where the stokers would be waiting.

There was some attempt to signal from the men in *Valiant* to the *Rodney* and from *Rodney* to *Hood* confirming that they would strike and demanding to know what *Hood* was doing. When the dinner party ended on board *Hood*, the Captains saw libertymen coming back to the *Hood* singing the 'Red Flag'. Commander McCrum had managed, by the exercise of considerable tact, to get them to board the ship in silence, but it was by persuasion rather than an exercise of disciplinary authority. Instead of going quietly below, the men assembled to discuss the situation on the forecastle. Harold Prestage, another RNVR man, wandered up out of interest, and wrote what he heard in an exercise book.

A stoker spoke, very emotional about keeping wife and two kids on three shillings a day. He said he owed ten pounds, how was he to pay? Several others spoke. They say we on the *Hood* are blacklegs and cowards, our people did not seem to support the crowd on shore much. At last after much haggling they decide to down tools at eight o'clock tomorrow morning.

Just before midnight, Tomkinson summoned Astley-Rushton. He was now considering cancelling the sailing after all. Astley-Rushton told him that the condition of the cruisers was satisfactory, but Tomkinson was aware, as he put in his report, that the battleships and his own flagship had men on board 'who intended to prevent their ships sailing the next morning'. Astley-Rushton talked him out of cancelling the sailing, urging him to 'bring matters to a head'. (Admiral Kelly later confirmed this, letter from Admiral Dornvile to Chatfield, CHT/2/2.) This was an extraordinary position to adopt: it is more conventional, if mutiny seems to be in the offing, to nip it in the bud than to bring it to a head. The fact that Tomkinson was acting on Astley-Rushton's advice was well known in the Fleet by the next day (Drage papers). 'It appeared probable,' Tomkinson later explained, 'that certain ships would proceed, and it was anticipated that if they did the others would follow.'

Astley-Rushton was not the ideal adviser in such a matter; none of his own cruisers were due to go to sea, and the battleships were not his responsibility. He resented Tomkinson's authority, and if there was going to be trouble in the battleships that would be Tomkinson's problem. He seems never to have considered that the trouble might spread to his cruisers.

Lieutenant-Commander Duckworth, in *Nelson*, later wrote in his journal, 'Fancy Tomkinson being left to deal with this, fancy him or anyone calling in Astley-Rushton for advice – and then taking it.'

Harold Prestage, the Royal Naval Volunteer Reserve boy in the *Hood*, went to sleep dreaming of fearful troubles. 'The crowd on the fo'c's'le, the hoarse orator, the cheers, the

dark, water lapping, the singing, the beams of the search-
light directed on the pier and canteen. It is all so strange.'
Robert Elkins, in *Valiant*, took the precaution of locking away
his sporting pistols before turning in, and Drage slept badly
('I'm really an awful coward'). At 1.20 in the morning,
Tomkinson, Senior Officer Atlantic Fleet, sent a signal to the
Admiralty which should have warned them how he wanted
them to act when trouble began.

> I am of the opinion that it may be difficult to get ships
> to sea for practice this morning, Tuesday. I have made
> the following general signal to the Atlantic Fleet in com-
> pany. Begins. The Senior Officer Atlantic Fleet is aware
> that cases of hardship will result in consequence of the
> new rates of pay. C.O.s are to make a thorough inves-
> tigation and report to me typical cases without delay in
> order that I may bring the matter at once to the notice
> of the Admiralty Message ends.

On no ship did any officer take measures to hinder the men
from striking.

6

Strike!

The actual leaders are usually competent seamen.
Lieutenant-Commander C. Drage,
'Some Modern Naval Mutinies', Conclusion

At 5.45 on Tuesday morning, Wincott went up onto the forecastle of the *Norfolk* and looked around. He thought of himself as the leader of action on his own ship and its initiator in the Fleet, and he was expecting to see some sign that the battleships were in disarray. Perhaps there might be cheering, or signalling. There was nothing. He had told everyone else that they would muster on the forecastle at six: now he was filled with the terrible suspicion that everyone else had proved to be full of wind, and that he would simply lead his own band of brothers straight to a pointless Court Martial. He came back down deeply disappointed, and announced that there was no point in taking any action, at least until after breakfast. 'I'm not going through this to hold the baby for other people' (Hill).

Out by the mouth of Cromarty Firth, *Repulse* was preparing for sea. *Repulse* had a crew that had only been together for two weeks, and was a long way from the rest of the Fleet. She sailed at 6.30 as planned. But as she began to move, booing began to rise from the battleships. Wincott had got it wrong.

In fact by the time that Wincott had taken his look around the Fleet it was already obvious to some officers in *Hood*, *Nelson*, *Rodney* and *Valiant* that they had real trouble on their hands. But a ship is a closed community, and no crew could know for sure that they were not alone, or that action was proceeding along similar lines in the other ships. What had been planned was a protest action that would embrace the entire Fleet. What actually happened was that each ship experienced its own separate strike.

In *Rodney*, the first real sign of trouble came at 5.15 in the morning, when the Petty Officer who routed out the boys found that he was getting no response. When some of the boys began to rise, sailors shouted to them to stay where they were. Others took delight in telling the Petty Officer exactly where he could go, knowing that they were safely protected by the seamen and stokers.

Men were supposed to fall in at six o'clock, but on *Valiant* they stayed where they were, in bed. Even the marines refused to get up.

> In the marines' mess deck nobody knew what it was for. Everybody just stopped in their hammocks or stayed in the mess-decks. There were no orders, it just happened. When the bugle came round, sounding off 'Reveille', nobody moved.
>
> There was nobody getting out of the marines' mess-deck until the actual Captain of Marines, Captain Fielding, came round every man individually – 'On the quarter deck!' Of course we had to go, we were sworn men, there's no comparison between a Naval man and a marine.
>
> After our Captain of Marines got us out the Commander, he went, the Lieutenant-Commander went round the seamen's mess-deck; they just jeered him out of the mess-deck. The only two officers who did anything at all was Lieutenant-Commander Drage, who was a very nice person, and Lieutenant Ralfs of the marines. In actual fact Lieutenant Ralfs was taking his neck in his own hands by going in to the seamen's mess because they had no time for the marines. He went in,

spoke reasonably to them and they gradually drifted along to clear lower-deck [Masters].

Someone had scrawled 'Cancelled' across the Daily Orders on the Ships Company Notice Board [Drage diary].

The Captain of the *Valiant*, Captain Scott, decided to take matters into his own hands and address the men as they reluctantly and leisurely ambled on to the quarter deck. He was well aware of the importance of the moment: if the *Valiant* did not go to sea, other ships would probably not go either. Scott was an elderly gentleman who had little know-ledge or understanding of his crew, and he misjudged the mood utterly. He told the men that they would have to put up with the cuts, that his pay was being cut too, and that if they could not manage on their money, they would have to send their wives out to work. There was a roar of protest. *Valiant* would not be sailing.

There had been some reluctance on the part of a few men to join the strike. John Preston, for example, a young AB, was told that he would be thrown over the side if he did not join in – he was frightened of getting a black mark on his record. Once the Captain had spoken, there seems to have been no need for further intimidation.

'Reveille' was met with the same inertia in *Rodney*. The seamen sealed the hatches and cut off the engine room to prevent the stokers getting up steam for sailing. The boilers had been due to light up at 5.30, but the Engineering Officer found his stokers in the smoking room instead of at work.

In *Nelson*, too, the stokers were out. They went up to the forecastle, passing through the seamen's mess-deck on the way and bringing many seamen with them. Bert Fordham, a marine, made his way to the 'heads' (the lavatory), which meant coming up through a hatchway in the foredeck. He popped his head up to find himself in the middle of a crowd of men standing earnestly on the forecastle with their hands raised. They were giving a show of hands to indicate that they did indeed mean to prevent the ship from sailing. Not being too sure of how a marine might be welcomed at this moment, he ducked quickly back down.

At 6.30 forty men in *Nelson* were still on their mess-decks, talking and leaning against lockers. William Symons, for example, was nicely comfortable when he found himself face to face with a Regulating Petty Officer (a ship's policeman).

> Crushers, we used to call 'em. He was with an officer by the name of Lieutenant-Commander Boatel. He came directly up to me and said, 'Symons, get up on deck.' So I just simply ignored him. 'Take his name.'

Symons would have cause to regret this brief moment of personal rebellion. It marks one of the different ways in which action was being taken in different ships. In some ships, men would obey no orders except those given individually and by name. In others they would obey any order except a sailing order. In the *Nelson*, the officers had been temporarily supplanted. The crew simply shrugged them off. There was no violence because there was no need for violence. The *Nelson* had gone to bed in the hands of its officers, and woken in the hands of its crew. Such are the dangers of a well-run ship.

The *Hood* was a happy ship, but not so well-run, and there was not quite the same air of efficiency about the start of the strike. Hargreaves, a second-class stoker, was due to go down and help to flash up the boilers at about 5.30 in the morning.

> I was stopped from going down the boiler room. I was stopped by a big stoker. He said 'get back' and I said 'No!' and he said 'Won't you?' and I looked at him and that was it. The ship had been taken over, otherwise he wouldn't have dared say it.

Men gathered on the forecastle, and at about 7.30 they were cheered by the men on *Rodney*. They cheered back.

Commander McCrum came on to the forecastle of the *Hood* and began to address the men. Harold Prestage's journal noted what happened.

> He is well liked by the men. He said, 'Lads, I am afraid I can do nothing for you, any special case of hardship will be looked into, I will do my best for you.' It must have been a pretty stiff ordeal for him. The men cheer him. He goes, a large part of the men go with him. The rest yell out, 'Come back, if we do not strike now they will crush us!' Part go back. I go to my gun. I am the only one on duty.

At eight o'clock the marine bands began to play the National Anthem while the men on all the ships in harbour stood to attention. As soon as colours were hoisted, a cheer began to pass from ship to ship around the anchorage. The awful truth was now visible to the officers on every ship.

Had they been reasonably aware of what was happening, they should have anticipated that *Valiant* might go on strike. If they were particularly prescient they might have expected (and some did) the four ships due to sail to take action together. What they had not expected at all was that Monday's experience ashore had created a common purpose throughout the Fleet. The whole of the Atlantic Fleet in harbour was in this together.

The actual situation in each ship varied greatly over the next few hours. The cruisers were in an odd position: their crews were going on strike before they were actually being asked to go to sea, so that all the men could do was demonstrate their solidarity with the larger ships by standing on the forecastle and cheering to them. The great variety of responses by the different Captains indicates that the cruiser squadron officers had been given no lead on how to handle such a situation – that it came, in fact, quite out of the blue as far as they were concerned.

The Captain of *Adventure* was evidently shattered by what was happening in his ship. When hands had been ordered to fall in, in the normal way, first thing in the morning, very few had done so. One of the small group who had obeyed the order was Harry Ackland.

> They didn't give us a duty, strange to relate. They sent us forrard. I distinctly remember this. And when we went forrard the older people said, 'Now look, you're out of turn, like. If you do anything like this again. . .You've laughed with the crowd, now cry with the crowd.' That was the saying I was told – 'You've laughed with the crowd, now cry with the crowd.' So I didn't fall in no more.

Evidently Captain Dibben had hoped that the few loyal men would talk their comrades back into obedience, but he could not compete with the authority of the three-badge Able Seamen. Once colours had been hoisted, the *Adventure* was plainly out of control.

> Everybody cheered, and you was trying to spell out the name of the nearest ship, which for us was *Rodney*. 'R–O–D–N–E–Y RODNEY! ARE YOU WITH US?' And then you'd get the answer back. And the next ship down the line would cheer. A tremendous cheer from each ship.
>
> Now normally that wouldn't happen, you see. You wasn't allowed to do that sort of thing.
>
> There was a bunting tosser [a semaphore signaller] stood up on the capstan and he had flags, and they had an Aldis lamp also, in between the two cable holders. But the Aldis lamp was held low and people was stood round the Aldis lamp, whereas the chap that was doing the technical semaphore was stood up on the capstan doing it openly.
>
> We didn't see any officers. The rumour went round that the marine that was on guard on the quarter deck

had a fixed bayonet. Now that was only a rumour, but they was laughing and chaffing to see if they would go aft and see this marine and say, 'Go on then, dig me, I'm your chum,' like. But they definitely said that the keyboard sentry had fixed bayonets.

What happened then was this. They said 'Clear Lower-Deck', you see. Now the answer was, 'If the Captain wants to see us, let him come forrard.' He didn't go on the fo'c's'le but he came forrard into the recreation room, you see. He didn't actually come on the fo'c's'le with the crowd. And I'll swear to this day that that Captain was crying. I was quite close to the Captain. I'll swear he was crying.

He gave us a lot of hubbabballar. People just didn't take any notice – they just didn't take any notice. And the Captain, the Master-at-Arms and the Duty Officer, they just walked aft.

Captain Custance, in the *York*, took a firmer line. Trouble had been slower starting in his ship, possibly because of the effect of the Commander's dramatic rescue dive the previous night. Ernest Lingham, on watch that morning, knew that the day had started normally and thought that nothing would come of all the talk after all. He was on duty as a telegraphist.

Everything seemed to be normal. At eight o'clock in the morning, which would be my time for going back on duty, they had been doing physical exercises and I thought all the talk was a lot of tommy-rot. Then I heard a lot of cheering. I went down to the wireless office, and to my amazement the next thing I heard was a lot of stamping and everybody stamping and cheering and this mutiny had started. It rather took me aback.

Lingham's explanation of the cheering reveals something of the character of this 'mutiny' – an act of loyal disobedience, schizophrenic in the attempt to take illegal action without breaking the bounds of legitimacy – an impossible, ridiculous posture which grew out of the deep affection of men for the Navy and, in ships like the *York*, for their officers and their ships.

There was a previous mutiny at the Nore [in the eighteenth century], when the signal for mutiny was whistling. That's why whistling is forbidden in the Navy. You're not allowed to whistle on any ship. No warship allows any whistling to take place. So this time, cheering was to be the signal.

Everybody packed up and that was it. The skipper then came forrard and said he'd like to speak to the men. Instead of facing him, they turned their backs on him. So he said then, 'Right, run the hoses.' So everybody said, 'You'll be be a very, very foolish man if you turn those hoses on – and who's going to run them anyway?' Then I realised what a spot the Petty Officers and Chief Petty Officers were in, because they were between the devil and deep blue sea. I thought, 'Now if he orders the Chief or a Petty Officer, which man's going to stand to oppose him?' But fortunately for him, he never gave that order. He treated them as men, and back he went aft.

Then I went on shift. I heard a lot of clanking and banging. He'd armed the marines. I asked one of the marines, 'What's all this about?' He said, 'We've had orders to guard the ammunition lockers, spirit room and magazine keys.' So I said, 'Nothing else?' He said, 'Well, no one's to come past us.' Well, I had to get back on shift. And this marine pointed a gun at me.

I said, 'Don't be a bloody fool. I've got to get back. Don't be so stupid.' I pushed his bayonet aside and he laughed, you know – but, I mean, there was a show if necessary.

According to the Captain's report, men refused to leave the forecastle until the marines were moved up one side of the ship towards them, allowing them room to escape down the other side. According to the accounts of the men concerned, things did not proceed quite as smoothly as that.

> Having proceeded as directed the officer in charge of the marines told the ratings to leave the forecastle and return to duty, alternatively he would have to order the marines to remove them.
>
> The reply to this ultimatum was that should he attempt anything of that nature he would ultimately be short of one marine detachment. After deliberating for a while the lieutenant ordered the marines to 'pile' arms in the sick bay flat and returned to the quarter deck [W. Knight, letter, supported by D. Whiteside, letter].

The crowd on *York*'s forecastle was quite small, however, and those who went aft as ordered were given a rather confusing lecture by Captain Custance, which included reference to the official explanation of the cuts, to the meaning of the Articles of War, and to the possibility that if men could produce evidence of a job ashore they would be allowed to leave the Navy.

The *York* had been quietened down – there would not be any cheering from her forecastle for the rest of the day – but little work was going to be done aboard.

In the *Norfolk*, Wincott realised at about 7.30 that the promised action was actually beginning to happen: *Valiant*'s launch was left dangling half-hoisted from her derrick, *Rodney* and *Adventure* had crowds on their forecastles. He went through the mess-decks announcing that they too should go up to the forecastle, and demanding that the marines should also take part. Meanwhile men who had not been at the meeting in the recreation room on Monday night were wandering about asking what they were supposed to do. A group of older men who had formed around Wincott began issuing orders: everyone, including stokers and marines, was to go forward, with the marines in the very bows of the ship, hidden from their officers by a wall of ratings.

To begin with, the marines, not knowing where they stood, barricaded themselves in their barracks:

> The Captain of Marines came to try to get them out. I forget the First Lieutenant's name now, but I think it was Langton and he was a well-liked man. He could work anywhere he wanted on that ship without fear or favour: he was the First Lieutenant, and he was the one that tried to stop the Captain of Marines from going through the bulkhead doors. Because he said, 'If you go through there they'll kill you!' And those were the words that were used [Wood].

The marines went up from their barracks to join the crowd on deck.

> I was standing quite close to the Royal Marines, and the Sergeant Major and the Sergeant was doing their best to get the Royal Marines to turn to again. And they failed. So the Captain of the Marines was brought onto the scene. And he decided to use his method which was – he picked out a man and named him, said to him, 'You, so-and-so, will turn to and not let the side down.' All the time he was speaking we kept our heads bowed, just to show that we were not interested in what was being said.
>
> Well, when the Royal Marines refused to answer yes or no, the Sergeant Major lost his temper, I'm afraid. He sprung to attention, took a couple of paces forward, a smart salute and said to the Captain of Marines, 'Shall I place him under arrest, sah!' And he was told very quickly, 'You'll do nothing of the sort. If the man wants to be a mutineer, that's entirely up to him.' Had such a thing have happened, there'd have been a riot, never mind a mutiny [Hill].

The Captain had attempted to address the men, summoning them aft to listen to a lecture on the need for the cuts and the parlous economic state of the nation: it was an ill-conceived speech which bored many, angered a few and was incomprehensible to almost all: they drifted away and left him marooned, his authority evaporating in the autumn wind.

The *Norfolk* was the only ship where one individual, Wincott, clearly tried to take charge of the action; in other ships there was a feeling that everyone had made a mass decision, though of course some men were prominent in arguing for it and seeing it through. In the *Norfolk*, Wincott's personal enthusiasm for leadership produced something closer to a conventional image of mutiny. He was acting as a usurping authority, with his own staff of 'linkmen' imposing that authority by force where they felt it was necessary.

> Down below decks some of them was arguing the point and didn't want to join it, you know; that's when there were one or two beatings, good hidings, fights. Grady was a leading stoker and he was in a fight, with one of the ringleaders, a seaman who had about eighteen months left to do. Grady was a smashing feller, he was about twenty-six and was waiting to be made Leading Seaman. Joining the strike would have put him back no end, you know, because he wouldn't have been recommended. That was one of the reasons he didn't want to join. He had a good hiding in the night. In the morning you could see it, too, because he had a couple of black eyes to go with it [Wood].

Grady's scruples would not have cut much ice with Wincott: he too had passed his Leading Seaman's examination and was waiting for promotion.

The only ship where the men were talked back to duty was the *Dorsetshire*, flagship of the cruiser squadron. There had been a widespread refusal to turn out at six o'clock, and those who did fall in were told of Tomkinson's signal to the Admiralty and promised that hardships would indeed be investigated. Astley-Rushton then asked these men to go and spread that information, while the marines were kept out of harm's way on the quarter deck.

At first this policy yielded no results: the *Dorsetshire*'s men remained on the forecastle and cheered with the rest of the Fleet. The Captain went on to the forecastle and said that if they would come aft he could get on with investigating their grievances: no result. The Padre then tried but was told that, having gone this far, they might as well be hung for a sheep as a lamb and stay on strike.

The Captain saw his opportunity. He went forward again and strongly implied that if they now returned to duty, having made their point, he could treat them sympathetically, but if they remained on the forecastle there was nothing more they could achieve except endangering their jobs, their pensions and their prospects. Feeling that they had indeed made their gesture and been let off the hook, the crowd on the forecastle dispersed. Perhaps a letter from one of the men in *Dorsetshire* expresses more clearly than any commentary the way many of these seamen thought and felt about things.

> Some of the Lads stopped in the Messdeck and some went on the forecastle, after a while the Padre came up with one of the Officers and spoke to us all, and the trip we were going on that was Sweden, Denmark and Hamburg and it would be the first ship since 1914 to go there, so we got under way then. We went to all these places and had a wonderful time, if you had a Daily Sketch of 1932 I think you would see some of the Lads going round in chairaplanes on the fair at Hamburg. . .I only wrote to you to let you know what ships I was on and a good crowd of Officers and men we had on all the ships I was on, I still think of them and the good time we had.

The action being taken on the cruisers was essentially one of solidarity with the big ships: those were the ships that were due to sail. In the *Valiant*, the marines had gone into the bows of the ship, as in *Norfolk*, to avoid being recognised and given a direct order. The Captain of Marines had very nearly sparked a serious incident by putting on his revolver and going to some of the marines' barracks, but he was restrained and told to be more careful. The stokers had refused to get up steam: some steam was raised by Petty Officers, but not enough to proceed safely to sea. No attempt was made to take charge of the situation by the Captain or Commander: it was simply reported to Tomkinson at 8.47 that it was not safe under these circumstances to put to sea.

The complete absence of any serious attempt to control the situation on the big ships is one more indication that there was a deliberate policy of leaving events to take their own course. *Nelson* and *Rodney* were due to sail at 9.30. *Rodney* was in a state of complete chaos: there was no strike organisation at all, just a general refusal to work. The officers made a move to get the ship away by slipping the cable that held her to the mooring buoy, but with men sitting on the cable and with their arms and legs through the links this was not a serious proposition: besides, the stokers had shut down most of the power. Everyone was on strike, even the cooks, and it took some hurried discussion on the forecastle to make sure that meals and other services essential to life would still be maintained. Some of the Leading Seamen and even Petty Officers joined in the process of setting up the necessary organisation. The men were allowed complete freedom to get on with their mutiny: they even lowered ropes through the hatchway into the recreation room, and hauled the piano up onto the forecastle. For the next two days, the cheery sound of *Rodney*'s piano would be a signal to the whole Fleet that the strike was still going on.

Just before seven in the morning, the Captain of *Nelson*, Captain Burges-Watson, had decided to address his men.

I don't think for one moment he meant it in the way that it was accepted, but his words were very ill-chosen. He said, 'Well, now is the time for your wives to do something.' Well at that time, of course, women didn't work, and it was taken as 'Well, now your wife will have to go out and take a man or two.' I think that's the way it was taken by the crew. And there was a rumbling.

He got down, and I was standing quite close, he turned round to Commander Lake and he said, 'I'm going to my cabin, Lake, the men are yours.' And we never saw him again throughout the whole incident [C. H. Williams].

This story expresses a number of important features of what was taking place. First, there is no mention of the men being urged back to work, or even reference to possible punishment for what they were doing. This is common to all the accounts from *Hood, Rodney, Valiant* and *Nelson*. Second, there is a total collapse of authority on the part of the Captain. An isolated, lonely figure, not at all well known among the thousand or more men on board, his authority over the crew is obviously purely nominal – a fact which is made very plain when he has to try to exercise it in a crisis. Many of the Captains were genuinely weak men anyway; the Captain of *Rodney* pleaded with his men for a return to work, or, failing that, would they please let him have his messenger boy back. The men, contemptuous, left it to the boy to decide.

The real figure of authority and command on board is the Commander, and it is evident that the quality of a ship's company depended on him. Lake was well able to handle the situation, within the limits that were evidently in force.

I can see him stood up there with his telescope, everybody cheering, 'Hallo, Lou Lake', then everybody quietened down and he said, 'I don't blame you chaps for what you're doing.' They were his actual first words. Of course everybody cheered. Cheering died down. He said, 'But I'd ask you fellers to remember that there are officers in this Fleet and this ship who have had their salaries docked every year. Don't look at me – my salary doesn't pay my mess bill. But you know the officers on this ship, and they haven't been able to do anything about it. It's been docked every year.

'But you fellers, it's come as a sudden shock to you, and I can understand how you feel. Now those of you who are suffering as a result of this, I want you to write it down on a piece of paper, don't give it to anybody: I shall leave my cabin window open and just drop it through, so I don't know who it is. I want to collect all these together so I've got something to show how much you are suffering.'

That is how Charles Williams remembers it, and others have given similar accounts. It is interesting that Lake was able, in their recollection, to appeal to men's feelings for the officers at such a moment, and to base his approach on confidence in his own popularity. When he had first come into the ship he had found discipline slack, with men dropping cigarette ends on deck. In his early days on board he had made a sandwich-board and when he saw a man drop a cigarette butt, he made him wear the board as a mark of shame. If that man saw another commit the same offence he was to pass the board on. At first such techniques were resented, but not for long; Lake was prepared to commit himself to the ship and expected everyone else to do the same, with remarkable results. That was how he had made the *Nelson* into the winning ship in the regatta, Cock of the Fleet, holder of the prized silver chanticleer.

Finally, in this examination of Charles Williams's account, there is the mention of the fear of the married men that their wives might take to prostitution.

The tensions placed on married life by long periods at sea – up to two-and-a-half years on a foreign commission – were very great. The married men had plenty of reason to be worried about the security and stability of their marriages before the cuts in pay: now they were having nightmares. No amount of loyalty and affection for the ship, the Navy or the officers could counterbalance these fears, among men who well knew from their own behaviour the frailty of human nature.

Not knowing what might happen next, the forecastle party in *Nelson* lashed up the anchor cables, and made heaps of stanchion bolts on deck, to repel any attempt to free the cables by force. None came. One officer wanted to call out the marines, but Lake confined him to his cabin. The marines had taken the precaution of hiding in lockers.

By nine o'clock Tomkinson had come to the conclusion that the Admiralty could be told that the situation he had warned of had come to pass. His signal read:

> Situation 0900 today. HMS *Repulse* has proceeded to sea for exercises other ships have not and considerable portions of ships companies have absented themselves from duty attitude of all ratings towards their officers is at present correct. I have recalled ships out exercising and stopped leave of officers and men Chief of Staff leaving here today arriving Admiralty early tomorrow morning.

There are a number of details here which perhaps deserve comment. At 0900 only one ship besides *Repulse* was due to have sailed, and that was *Valiant*. Originally, *Hood* had been due to go out at the same time as *Repulse*, but during the weekend Tomkinson had moved its sailing time to ten o'clock without informing the Admiralty (there was, after all, no reason why he should inform them). The implication is clearly that Tomkinson was not expecting his officers to resolve the situation, but was recognising the strike as a *fait accompli*. Elkins, in *Valiant*, noted the wardroom feeling:

> It was. . .a matter for argument why the officers had not in the first place been allowed to deal with the outbreak in the way that it merited. . .It was argued that at any moment, if all those who were loyal in the ship were armed and sent forward, the whole thing would subside. It seemed that the policy adopted in

each ship had been the same and could only be accounted for by order from some superior officer.

That was, and remains, Drage's view too. It is also curious that Tomkinson should have recalled the ships out exercising (actually he had not done that yet: his recall signal went out at 09.31). In the light of what was happening, it seems absurd to recall ships unaffected by mutiny to a disaffected Fleet. No explanation was ever offered for this order, except for the possibility that had it not been done men might have suspected that there was a plot to split up the Fleet. Perhaps the likeliest explanation is that Tomkinson believed that the trouble would all be over by the time those ships came in. He had told the Admiralty overnight that he was holding an investigation into the hardships caused by the cuts. If the whole Fleet was gathered together that investigation could take place more easily, and given a quick reply now from the Admiralty, saying that the cuts could be reviewed, there would be no further trouble.

If this was indeed the way Tomkinson was thinking, he had made a serious error. He had underestimated the scale of unrest in his Fleet, and overestimated the speed with which the Admiralty might react. In fact when he did get a reply, a little after midday, it offered no concessions.

Their Lordships entirely approve of the action you have taken. Any representations which you think it right to make as a result of your investigations will be carefully considered by the Board. Meanwhile officers should also take every opportunity of laying stress on the fact that great sacrifices are being required from all classes of the community and that unless these are cheerfully accepted the financial recovery of the country will be impossible. Similar changes of pay have been made in the Army and Royal Air Force.

Which was really no help at all.

7

Living with Mutiny

> After the first explosion, this 'Mutiny Atmosphere'
> tends to burn itself out.
>
> Lieutenant-Commander C. Drage,
> 'Some Modern Naval Mutinies', Conclusion

At 9.31 a.m., Tomkinson signalled that the exercises were cancelled: *Malaya*, *Warspite*, *Repulse* and the target tug *St Cyrus* were to return to harbour, and *Valiant* was to remoor. The remooring required a certain amount of tact: as the boys and Petty Officers began to work on the cable, the sailors assumed that this was another attempt to get the ship to sea. They lined up by the kedge anchor, and threatened to release it if work on the cables did not stop. The kedge anchor was an emergency device, easy to drop but complicated to get up again: unlike the main anchors, its capstan could not be worked by steam and required a large number of men. The cable officer explained what was happening and pacified the hands, and they went back to the forecastle to watch their officers in unaccustomed toil.

On each ship an attempt was now being made to investigate men's grievances over the cuts, so that the Chief of Staff would have a satisfactory dossier to take with him when he left on the lunchtime train.

Now that the immediate crisis had passed without either violence or a break in solidarity, each ship began to follow its own distinctive pattern of life. In *Nelson*, where the men were quite confident of their position, the normal work of harbour routine continued as though nothing had happened. The older men who were taking responsibility for the action held their own meetings and discussed the position with the Commander. The only sign that there was anything unusual was the constant crowd of men on the forecastle, cheering at intervals to show that they were still refusing to go to sea. In the *York*, where a show of force had shaken a number of the crew, there was not even a forecastle gathering any longer: after all, the *York* had no sailing orders to strike against.

In *Valiant* and *Rodney*, however, a normal harbour routine was being ignored. There had been a complete collapse of official authority, and on these ships the informal authority of the older men was not strong enough to take over. John Sampson remembers the mutiny in *Rodney* as a holiday.

> We spent the rest of the day till dinner time on the upper deck, joining in with the lads, cheering the ships in the Fleet. We came down to dinner, and then in the afternoon volunteers were called for; the baker needed flour and asked for volunteers to go to the stores, and the galley wanted meat, so volunteers were called for to bring up the meat from the cold store room. They were never short of volunteers.
>
> They were playing the piano, a bit of a sing-song, they played the 'Red Flag' very often. Leaders stood up on the fo'c's'le with some of the crew around, giving morale-boosting speeches. 'Stick together – we don't want this pay cut – if we all stick together they're bound to give in eventually.' That was the theme. Then they would call for three cheers across to the nearest ship.

Few men were persuaded to help in the hardship investigations on board *Rodney* or *Valiant*.

Adventure was in a similar state, with orders being piped but only responded to by cheering from the forecastle. In *Norfolk*, Wincott and his committee of linkmen ensured that necessary work was done, but in the words of one man, 'links between the officers and men were severed'. The extraordinary form which the mutiny had taken in *Norfolk* created a unique response when men were asked to state their grievances. George Hill, who seems to have been used as a constant go-between for communication with the men, was asked to make out a statement of grievance: Hill maintains that he was told by Lieutenant-Commander Rodgers that the Captain needed such a document urgently and was in despair. Hill went to ask Wincott if it was all right for him to oblige.

> When I approached Wincott, his remarks were 'I'll give him a statement. Clear Lower Deck! Everybody on the fo'c's'le!' In a moment of panic, as you might say, you'd have thought it was abandon ship, there was a mad rush to get onto the fo'c's'le deck. When Wincott and I got onto the fo'c's'le deck, looking across the bridge deck from port to starboard there was nothing but officers. And there was still an overflow of officers who came down on to B gun deck. That left the fo'c's'le deck clear for men to stand around and listen to the proceedings.

A table, typewriter and chair were brought, and the entire company watched while Leonard Wincott dictated and George Hill typed a document which bears comparison with the petition of the Nore mutineers in the Revolutionary Wars; a petition which resulted in bringing a great number of eighteenth-century mutineers to the hangman's noose.

> I must make it clear that when we started off I had no experience of taking down dictation, neither had Wincott any idea of how to address me or give over his dictation. I made a total mess of the whole proceedings, much to my aggravation, so I had to take everything out of the machine, tear it up in bits and throw it away and start all afresh. Now this time I didn't want the same results, so I said to Wincott, 'You tell me what

102

you want to say, and leave it to me. Above all, please speak a little slower.'

And thus, with Wincott slowly dictating on the inspiration of the moment, and Hill polishing the phrasing and grammar as he went, they produced a manifesto for their mutiny.

'We, the loyal subjects of H.M. the King, do hereby represent to My Lords Commissioners of the Admiralty our representations to implore them to amend the drastic cuts in pay that have been inflicted upon the lowest paid man of the lower deck. It is evident to all concerned that this cut is the forerunner of tragedy, misery and immorality amongst the families of the lower deck, and unless we can be guaranteed a written agreement from Admiralty, confirmed by Parliament, stating that our pay will be revised, we are still to remain as one unit, refusing to serve under the new rate of pay.'

Now at that point Wincott stopped speaking and I asked him, 'Carry on'. He said, 'That is all I've got to say'. Now that didn't please me one bit, because to my impression what he had said was more or less a command or an order – take it or else! It didn't give anything away in any shape or form. So I felt there was only one thing to do.

Hill added a sentence of his own. 'Men are quite willing to accept a cut which they, the men, consider to be fair and just.' Wincott later claimed to be baffled at what mistaken urge had led him to add this compromising sentence: if Hill is correct, Wincott need worry no longer – he didn't write it at all. Eight copies were duplicated. One was put in Rodgers's cabin. Another found its way to the *Daily Herald*. Some were distributed surreptitiously around the Fleet by the *Norfolk*'s boat crew in the course of carrying mail and official messages. In the *Norfolk* souvenir copies were made by a calligrapher.

Once the demonstration had been made, there was

nothing for the Fleet to do but wait. There was regular cheering throughout the day from ship to ship, with the exception of *Dorsetshire* and *York*, accompanied by covert ('short-arm') semaphore signalling and, until, it was cut off in mid-morning, some signalling by telegraph, but these signals really had no content beyond 'Still holding out OK'. Officers continued to be served their meals in their ward-rooms, boys continued to receive instruction, and on all ships except the *Valiant*, *Rodney*, *Norfolk* and increasingly *Adventure*, normal harbour duties were carried out. The solidarity that had been forged in the canteen had been limited to stokers and seamen: marines and Petty Officers were not asked to take any part in the strike except for the marines in *Valiant* and *Norfolk*, where they did join in. But it is quite clear that the marjority of all non-commissioned ranks, from Artificer Chief Petty officers to boy seamen, felt that the strike was, in the circumstances, right and necessary. There were, of course, individuals at every level who believed that what was happening was utterly wrong, but their numbers were only significant in the three newly-commissioned ships.

In *Hood*, *Nelson*, *Dorsetshire* and *York* a rapid collection of hardship statements was put together for the Chief of Staff, Rear-Admiral Colvin, to take to London. Some of the accounts they received made a deep impression: as the Captain of *Nelson* noted in his report, for some men the cuts meant not hardship, but ruin.

Colvin and his secretary set out for London at about one in the afternoon, to the cheers and jeers of the men on the forecastles. Colvin made the best of the situation, waving cheerily to *Rodney*'s men as he passed. Everyone assumed that now the men had shown that they would not tolerate unjust treatment, the Admiralty would quickly recognise the error of its ways.

The Admiralty's midday signal, when it came, was not at all what Tomkinson had hoped for. While he was pleased enough to be told that the Admiralty approved of his actions, Tomkinson was after some more concrete help from them. At twenty minutes to two, he therefore sent an explanation of the problem, which he listed as

> a) the extent of the cuts of pay of leading rates and below who were on the old scale.
> b) the short interval before reductions take effect.
> c) alleged affirmation by Government on several occasions that ratings on the old scale would continue to receive it during the whole period of service. . .
> I do not consider that the men will feel they have received justice unless reductions are more in proportion to their pay e.g. the pay of an able seaman to be reduced by 6d instead of 1s.
> I would urge a very early decision should be communicated by their Lordships. Unless this is received I regret that in my opinion discipline in the Atlantic Fleet will not be restored and may still further deteriorate [ADM 178/129].

This was a correct and reasonable statement of the position – as correct and reasonable as Wincott's petition, if more specific. And like Wincott's petition, it amounted to an ultimatum. The phrasing of the final paragraph suggests that Tomkinson had not even realised that the pay cuts were a matter for the Cabinet. There was no reply.

Two hours later, *Malaya*, *Warspite* and *Repulse* came back into harbour. They were greeted with cheers.

Tomkinson's order that the Admiralty Letter should be explained had not been carried out in *Repulse*: it was one of the ships which had not received a copy of the letter. Instead, the crew were told while sailing back exactly what the cuts would mean, and were asked to make representations if they would suffer undue hardship. One of the men who did volunteer to speak to his Divisional Officer remembers being treated without much sympathy.

> I said I had to pay hire purchase on furniture: he said

I shouldn't have hire purchase, wait till you've got the money. I said I've never got the money. Then I said I've got to buy soap and tobacco. He said 'You shouldn't smoke'. Then I said I've got to go on leave – 'You shouldn't go on leave, stay aboard ship.' So I got no-where with him.

Sometimes a lack of sympathy was justified. The man who gave that account was a self-confessed trouble-maker who was spinning a yarn. He was simply interested to see if there was a chance of getting some advantage out of the situation. There were other men on board who had real cause for worry, but few of them wanted to discuss their families' problems with their officers. Ernest Eldred, for in-stance, was a torpedoman with two good-conduct stripes, plus marriage and child allowance, making a total income of £2 5s 3d a week: a cut of a shilling a day was certainly not 25 per cent, and so he expected little sympathy. But he remembered the promise that the old rate of pay was sac-rosanct, and felt bitterly betrayed. When he realised the state of the rest of the Fleet, he was certainly in a mood to join in.

That night a meeting was held on *Repulse*'s forecastle, at which a group of men decided to down tools. They were to receive encouragement from the rest of the Fleet.

The general feeling throughout the ship was one of anger, real anger at the cuts and the person that was doing the cuts, the First Lord of the Admiralty. It was bitter against him. A pinnace came round and there was several fellers in there. They shouted out through a megaphone, explaining what was happening and what not to do and what to do. If it was put in today's terms, it would be like a shop steward saying 'Brothers, we strike'. If I remember rightly the term 'Brothers' was mentioned. We gave them three cheers [E. F. Eldred].

The decision to join the strike was signalled that night by Aldis lamp to the rest of the Fleet.

Warspite and *Malaya* had to sail right into the heart of the Fleet to take up their positions. Admiral French in *Warspite* had known nothing of the trouble until Tomkinson's morning signal to the Admiralty was intercepted by his ship: the investigation of hardship cases had already begun in these two battleships, and he ordered their Captains to address their crews on what was happening and to remind them of the hardship investigations. The address that was given in *Warspite* was sufficiently obscure for the men not to realise what had happened in the Fleet until they came in and saw the crews of *Nelson* and *Valiant* yelling and cheering at them – believing, of course, that the ships coming in were being brought to join the mutiny by their crews, and not guessing that Tomkinson had actually ordered them to rejoin the Fleet. Once they realised that *Warspite* was not on strike, these men started yelling 'Windy *Warspite*' and broader terms of abuse. Conditions aboard *Warspite* were similar to those in *Repulse* and a number of men decided during the night that they would join the strike.

The Captain's address in *Malaya* had been something of a disaster. When he began to explain that he was putting up with a pay cut, so they could too, there was a growl of protest. The Commander took over and calmed the situation, while the Captain retired to his cabin. In effect, the Commander pre-empted the situation by leaving the men with nothing to strike against.

> He said we don't know quite what has happened at Invergordon, but we've got to go back, secure the ship and anchor. But once we get there I won't need any ordinary ship's duties carried out. You must clean up your messes, keep them clean, sweep down the upper deck once a day, and that'll be your duties. We, the officers, are all on your side. We'll fight to the very last for you [E. J. Godwin].

There was thus no call for anyone in *Malaya* to refuse duty, and it would have been downright embarrassing to go on the forecastle and cheer as though the ship was in a state of crisis. Despite shouts of 'Westoe scabs' and derisive cheers from the other ships, there was nothing the crew of *Malaya* could or would do to join the 'passive resistance', and the Commander thus earned his ship the semi-official nickname of 'the loyal *Malaya*'.

One other ship received the signal to join the Fleet at Invergordon, and that was the cruiser *Exeter*. She was a brand new ship working up to join the Fleet for the first time, and as she sailed into Cromarty Firth in the late afternoon, no one on board knew that there was anything amiss. When one naval ship passes another, the 'Still' is sounded on the bugle, and everyone freezes at attention. The Captain and crew of *Exeter* were astonished to find that as they sailed through the Fleet they were being cheered – they assumed that this was a warm, if extraordinary, greeting for their first day in the Fleet. Some men cheered back, and the sailors in the Fleet cheered all the harder, believing, of course, that the *Exeter* had been taken over by its crew and brought to join the demonstration. In fact the crew of the *Exeter* took no part at all in the affair.

Towards the end of the day men in a number of ships began to consider the possibility that they would have to tell the Admiralty themselves what they wanted. On board *Valiant*, and possibly on some other ships, the text of the *Norfolk* petition was read aloud and endorsed. (Diary of A. M. Lucas ELK/10.) Committees were formed in several ships, not to direct the strike but to represent the men to the Admiralty. On all ships, whether work was being done or not, the officers were still being listened to when they spoke to the men (which was rarely, and in some ships never), and were still being served their meals. The peculiar flavour of the event is perhaps indicated by the fact that, leave having been stopped, no one sought to go ashore apart from a small group in *Warspite* – and they were led by a telegraphist who appears to have been an undercover security agent. In *Hood* the cinema was rigged for the evening: in *Valiant* there was a concert on deck after supper. The piano still played on *Rodney*'s forecastle, and on the deck of *Norfolk* men stood around a wind-up gramophone.

That evening a new signal came from the Admiralty:

> The Board of Admiralty will give their earnest and immediate consideration to representations of hardship. Meanwhile you should impress on ships companies that existing rates of pay remain in force until 1st October and that Their Lordships confidently expect that the men of the Atlantic Fleet will uphold the tradition of the Service by loyally carrying out their duty [ADM 178/129].

By now the Press had wind of the story, and were trying to get some statement from the Admiralty: some newsmen were travelling to Invergordon overnight, and it would plainly be impossible to prevent the story getting out. Newspaper editors were therefore provided with an anodyne statement:

> The Senior Officer, Atlantic Fleet, has reported that the promulgation of the reduced rates of pay has led to unrest among a proportion of the lower ratings. In consequence of this he has deemed it desirable to suspend the programme of exercises of the Fleet and to recall ships to harbour while investigations are being made into representations of the hardship occasioned by certain of the cuts in pay, in order that these may be reported for the consideration of the Board of Admiralty.

Editors were told that they should avoid the use of the word 'mutiny' in their reporting.

It was a tense night for the officers of the Fleet. They well knew that their remaining authority was based on nothing more than the good will of the men, and the men's conviction that the demonstration would, with the good offices of their officers, have some effect. Although the initial moments of the demonstration had passed without any violence, and so far there had been no incidents of officers being threatened or of sabotage, tension was building up on the worst-affected ships. Events in these ships had also undermined the confidence of the junior officers in their superiors: Drage wrote anxiously in his diary,

> 'No steps are apparently being taken to deal with the mutiny; no guidance of any kind is being given to officers of any rank (or, for that matter, to Chief and Petty Officers).'

And it was plain that the Admiralty were not responding to the demands that were being made. At about the same time as the Press Release, the Admiralty sent a long signal to Tomkinson, which it repeated to all Commanders-in-Chief. This signal, number 914 in the Admiralty series of signals, was, in effect, a supplement to the Admiralty Letter, seeking to explain that the pay cuts were not really all that bad. It calculated that once allowances were taken into account, a seaman gunner with six years' service, receiving marriage allowance, would actually only lose 10 per cent of his pay. Apart from the irrelevance of this to the needs of the moment, it was also factually wrong. A married seaman gunner with six years' service would be under twenty-five years old, and would be ineligible for marriage allowance. The signal also demanded 'that programme of exercises should be resumed as soon as your investigations are complete.'

Tomkinson seems to have been in despair, and the Captain of the Fleet, Captain A. E. Evans, drafted a firm reply for him which was sent off just before one in the morning.

> I must emphasize that the situation at Invergordon will not be met until definite decisions have been communicated. A continuation of the Exercise programme is out of the question in the present state of mind of a

considerable proportion of the crews. Your 914 will be dealt with in further telegrams.

A signal was also sent to the Fleet, again in Tomkinson's name, pointing out that the Chief of Staff would arrive at the Admiralty in the morning, that no action could be expected for a day or two, and saying 'meanwhile I expect men to carry out duties'. This was the first general communication from Tomkinson to the Fleet since the exercises had been stopped, and it was clearly intended to convey to the men that their action would achieve its desired goal. Tomkinson made it perfectly clear, in his signals and in his later report, that he believed the men had an entirely just case and very little alternative open to them. But his appeal for a return to duty, in the absence of a tangible response from the Admiralty, was a lost cause. 'I'm not going to say the comments that was written on that when it was put on the notice board in *Nelson*, but it wasn't very good' (Williams).

The men themselves were generally a little tense, but not too worried. After all, this was the twentieth century: they were involved in a strike to claim their ordinary rights to a living wage. No one would hang them from the yard-arm. Some of them noted planes flying overhead, and speculated on the possibility that something nasty might be in the wind – but this was Britain, not Chile. No one would want to call down death onto them.

They could not guess how wrong they were.

8
To Crush or not to Crush?

At half past nine on Wednesday morning the Board of Admiralty met: they had an hour-and-a-half to prepare their advice to the Cabinet. Before looking at the issues they had to consider, we should take a look around the office of the First Sea Lord.

When Chamberlain had gone to Cabinet and accepted the cuts on the last day in August, he appears to have known little of the long history of the proposal to abolish the old rates of pay, and the bitterness which would be created if it were done. He was acting on inadequate advice – a politician dealing on his own account with a purely political question. As he later wrote, when the cuts had been agreed 'We were misled by the fact that men were already serving happily and contentedly on the new rates . . . our fears concentrated on the probable charge that we had broken faith; not on the individual hardships' (*Life of Sir Austen Chamberlain*, II, p. 383, Sir Charles Petrie (1940)).

Now he was suddenly at the centre of a major political crisis, and his adrenalin began to flow once more. 'I had no idea that my 'caretakers' job was going suddenly to become a centre of danger and interest' (ibid).

Chamberlain had been Civil Lord in 1895–1900, but knew nothing of the Navy now. His concern was with the great political issues. This crisis was a challenge to the emergency economic measures, and it was his job to save the nation.

His Board consisted of the Sea Lords, who were Admirals appointed for short terms of office, one other politician and the Permanent Secretary, Sir Oswyn Murray. The Permanent Secretary provided the only element of continuity, and Oswyn Murray had worked in the Admiralty since 1897.

The First Lord's principal adviser was supposed to be the First Sea Lord, Admiral Field. Field was generally known as 'Tam' and when younger had been popular because of his sense of humour, his ability to memorise names and his lack of ostentation. Now he was a sick man.

Field's assistant was Vice-Admiral Frederick Dreyer – Field was, by virtue of his office of First Sea Lord, the Chief of Naval Staff and Dreyer was his deputy. Dreyer, too, had been away on leave when Chamberlain was appointed and agreed to the pay cuts. He was fifty-three, seven years younger than Field and a much fitter man: he carried a great deal of Field's workload. He was a cold, humourless, precise and very brilliant man who was more interested in guns than in the men who worked them. He was austere and a stern disciplinarian.

The Second Sea Lord was Admiral Cyril Fuller: he was Chief of Naval Personnel, and had actually been on hand in the Admiralty when the pay cuts had been agreed. He had utterly failed to convey to Chamberlain their true significance and he was to suffer for it.

The Third Sea Lord, Admiral Backhouse, Controller of the Navy, which meant that he was fully absorbed in keeping the Navy's armament adequately supplied while coping with dramatic financial cuts. The Fourth Sea Lord, Preston, had protested vigorously at the proposals and offered his resignation, which was refused. As Chief of Supplies and Transport, he was anyway wrapped up in administrative detail.

There was one more politician on the Board, Earl Stanhope. There were supposed to be two, a Civil Lord and a Parliamentary Secretary: when Chamberlain took over, both of these were Labour Party men whose advice he would not have considered particularly helpful. The Civil Lord resigned almost at once and was not replaced: the Parliamentary Secretary hung on until the cuts had been accepted and then quit, to be replaced by Stanhope. Stanhope had served at the Admiralty before, and regarded the Naval members of the Board with contempt. Early in September, when he had just been appointed, he received a letter of congratulations from his old friend Admiral John Kelly, who was now retired on half-pay and was trying to get a job as Commander-in-Chief of the Atlantic Fleet or as Second Sea Lord. Stanhope's letter of reply is splendidly indiscreet.

> Thanks so much for your letter. It is a great joy to be back in office again and in the old Department, but these cuts are hateful.
>
> I wish to God you were at the Admiralty. I am sure there are several ways we can save money and perhaps *gain* in efficiency, but you know what this Board is. *I* think it is far the worst I have ever served with. 1st and 4th S.L.s and D.C.N.S. have been and I believe still are on leave (though I think 4th S.L. came back yesterday before his leave was up). Meanwhile pay and allowances for the Fleet are perhaps being settled for this generation and heavy cuts are due. Yet the Sea Lords responsible are away!! Of course Backhouse is a tower of strength, but confines himself to his own department which is more than a whole time job.
>
> Personally I hope this Govt lasts only a few weeks. Otherwise the public will forget the socialist iniquities which have brought us to this *v* serious position and will only remember our cuts which are bound to be unpopular as they are widespread.

These, then, were the men who had to consider what to do. They knew that the story of the mutiny was in the morning papers, though it had little coverage yet from the Continental Press – perhaps decisive action could kill the whole matter before the foreign bankers began to panic. They did not yet know that in the United States newspaper stories were predicting that trouble would spread to the police and armed forces, and that a train of events had

begun which would destroy the government's financial policy come what may. They believed that the future of that
policy depended on what decision they took now.

They had seen the signals from Invergordon, which
clearly indicated that the Fleet would not submit to discipline
unless the pay cuts were altered. They listened to Admiral
Colvin's description of the situation, which reinforced the
points made by Tomkinson: in justification, Colvin pre-
sented some typical examples of the hardship cases collected
before he set out.

The minutes of this meeting have never been released to
the public. But in Admiral Dreyer's papers in Churchill College, Cambridge, there is an indication of what took place.

According to Dreyer's note (DRYR 8/1), 'lesser lights' than
Field among the Sea Lords were proposing that the Fleet
should be bombarded by heavy howitzers from beyond the
hills round the Cromarty Firth.

The document is one in which Dreyer is acting as a po-
lemicist, arguing that the First Sea Lord was in full command
of the situation. One wonders who, on that Board, would
have recommended such action. Backhouse was a sensible
man, who would seem unlikely to have recommended such
an incredible course: Preston, the Fourth Sea Lord, had
asked to resign over the cuts. Fuller, the Second Sea Lord,
was responsible for personnel and had failed to warn Chamberlain of the danger of abolishing the 1919 pay rates –
perhaps he seems the likeliest candidate. Dreyer himself
generally appears as the most hawkish member of the Board,
but he makes it plain that he regarded the idea of a howitzer
bombardment as 'wild'. That could, of course, have simply
been because he knew a great deal about weaponry. In
Chile, to avoid doing too much expensive damage to the
mutinous ships, the rebellious fleet had been attacked with
light bombs – an action which had attracted much interest.

Whatever form an attack might take, it is clear that there
were arguments being put forward by members of the Board
for a military assault on the Fleet.

Such a plan seems quite incredible, but there are indications that this idea had some approval at the very highest levels of government. Chamberlain had informed his brother Neville and Stanley Baldwin of the mutiny at noon the previous day, and directly after lunch the First Lord's Naval Secretary, Admiral Chetwode, had signalled the news to Balmoral, adding that the Admiralty would try to keep the story quiet (ADM 178/129). It appears that from then on, the King's staff at Balmoral were kept informed by telephone. A plan to launch a military assault on the Fleet, using marine artillery or Naval aircraft, would certainly require government approval: it would also mean that the King would need to be kept in the picture, as Lord High Admiral of the United Kingdom, and as a monarch who happened to regard the Navy as his first love and his private property.

In this connection, it is interesting to note that the King had dined on Tuesday night with a Captain S. R. Mallet. His dinner guests were usually more exalted: on 12 September he had entertained Lady Constance Cairns, the next night Viscount and Viscountess Dunedin were at his table. On the Wednesday he was to entertain Sir Victor Mackenzie, Baronet of Glenmuick. Captain S. R. Mallet, his sole guest on Tuesday, is something of a mystery figure – he does not exist in the Army or Navy lists, nor is he in the Indian Army. He may have been a neighbour, perhaps a shooting neighbour – the King's diary for this day says 'Shot at Balmoral' – but a diligent search has failed to produce his name in any list or directory. But we are now in territory where there are many documents missing from the public files, and where there has been a clear attempt to conceal what was happening. Given the nature of the plans under discussion, that is perhaps not surprising.

Admiral Field, the First Sea Lord, was an accomplished conjurer and member of the Magic Circle. He it was who produced a rabbit from his hat, and escaped from the arguments for violence. Field argued that there was a possible way out of the situation which had not been mentioned by

116

Tomkinson. The men had got themselves into a situation from which they apparently could not escape, and plainly they would not take their ships to sea for exercises, but they might well be prepared to sail directly back to their home ports. If Colvin and Tomkinson were right – and he believed they were – then the men were mainly concerned for their families, and the more moderate among them, who must have been the majority, would not resist the opportunity to get back to their wives and children.

If this was Field's own idea, it was a remarkable one: since there was apparently no one on the spot suggesting that the men might respond positively to it, the order was described by Commander Kenneth Edwards as a 'gamble' in his book on the mutiny in 1937. Dreyer tried to get that book dis-credited, and the letter in which he described this Board meeting was aimed at achieving that: he insisted that Field understood sailors so well that it was no gamble. Lady Murray, in a book written after her husband's death, took up the same point and insisted that Sir Oswyn would never have agreed with the proposal if he thought that it was a gamble. He was, she said, 'the last man in the world to approve a gamble, and he did whole-heartedly approve this action taken by the Board of which he was a member.'

On the face of it, however, it seems surprising that any Board members could be confident that they understood the psychology of sailors very well, given the mess they had got into. Unless, of course, they had some piece of information which has still to come to light.

At eleven o'clock, Chamberlain went to the Cabinet meeting and read out the telegrams which had been received from Tomkinson. The Cabinet were apparently prepared to sanction an attack on the mutineers, but Chamberlain told them that another possibility existed, and Field and Colvin were brought in. Colvin seems not to have had much faith in the idea of ordering the men to return to their home ports; the Cabinet minutes say that 'he reported that in the opinion of the Acting Commander-in-Chief the Fleet would not move until some concession was made'. He particularly stressed the deep sense of grievance of married men aged between twenty-two and twenty-five who were serving on the old rate of pay without marriage allowances, and who had launched themselves into family life and hire purchase agreements on the basis of the pronouncements of previous governments that their pay would not be cut. He also indicated that the early date at which the cuts came into effect had aggravated the situation.

In the middle of the meeting, a further signal came from Tomkinson, headed 'MOST IMMEDIATE'. It was taken straight into the Cabinet.

> I am of the opinion the situation will get entirely out of control unless an immediate concession is made. Suggest (a) that percentage cut in pay (without allowances) for ratings below P.O. be proportionately that of higher ratings (b) that marriage allowance be applied to those ratings under twenty-five who have married on old scale of pay. Further I recommend representative of Board visit me to discuss matters on the spot.

It seems clear from the phrasing of the Cabinet minutes that Chamberlain was not personally urging the Cabinet to hold back from using force: he left that to Field. The First Sea Lord, who was supposed to be Chamberlain's adviser, was left to argue the case himself, recommending in addition that the cuts should be deferred for a month while the hardship investigations went ahead in the home ports. Field later wrote to Admiral Beatty that he personally persuaded the Cabinet to accept the home ports order [Roskill papers/171B].

The Cabinet took a lot of persuading. The idea of postponing the cuts was quite unacceptable: once they began to yield to force, the whole scheme of government economies would be vulnerable. The Cabinet minute records: 'To announce a concession in one case (more particularly one which could be represented as a surrender to force) would

have incalculable consequences. The suggested postpone-
ment was therefore unacceptable' (CAB 23/68 169). There
was then a forceful argument as to whether or not the ships
should be withdrawn to their home ports; 'as desired by the
Sea Lords', say the minutes, carefully excluding Chamberlain. 'This was eventually agreed to on the understanding
that it was made clear that this was done in obedience to an
order from the Admiralty.'

The phrasing of the minute is curious: it can be read in a
number of ways, one of which suggests that the Cabinet
was acting in obedience to the Admiralty. Sir Maurice Hankey, the Cabinet Secretary, was not normally careless with
words, and there may perhaps be a hint here that Field was
representing the wishes of the Lord High Admiral in Balmoral. There were some members of the Cabinet who firmly
believed that whether or not the ships obeyed it, the home
ports order was a serious mistake, and that the only correct
course of action was to shoot down the sailors. According
to Dreyer, who constantly attacked the Cabinet in retrospect,
there were Ministers who were still saying after the Cabinet
meeting that

> 'we *must* have the money and wanted to refuse *any*
> concession being made and to resort *to shooting*. The
> First Sea Lord was present when this was said' [memo,
> CHT/2/2].

The *New York Times* reported on Thursday that J. H. Thomas,
Secretary for the Dominions and Minister for Unemployment wanted to 'make an example' of the mutineers instead
of allowing them 'to sovietize the British Navy.' Thomas had
been leader of the Railwaymen's Union for many years and
was one of the small group of Labour Ministers who had
followed MacDonald into the wilderness of the National
Government, earning the deep hatred of a union that felt
betrayed. The following day, the same paper referred to the
ending of 'talk from the reactionaries about the sinking of
ships or shooting the mutineers'.

There was evidently a significant pressure in the Cabinet for the use of force, but eventually it was agreed that consideration might be given to helping classes of men suffering from real hardship, so long as the Admiralty made equivalent cuts elsewhere.

The meeting lasted for over three hours: at the end of it the Admiralty received an even more worrying signal from the Fleet.

Again it was headed 'MOST IMMEDIATE'.

> Situation 1400 Fleet informed cabinet sitting at noon. More ships have ceased ordinary harbour work and men are massing on forecastles at intervals. Adjacent ships cheering each other. Interference with running machinery and forced inter-ship communication may be next step.

There was, perhaps, an element of blackmail in this: the Fleet was being told to expect positive results from the Cabinet meeting, and that was being passed back to the Cabinet. Although the signal was from Senior Officer Atlantic Fleet, it did not use the first person and was, in fact, the product of what one officer (Lt-Commander Duckworth, in the *Nelson*) called 'a soviet of Rear-Admirals'. At a few minutes after nine, Tomkinson had signalled to French and Astley-Rushton that he wanted to see them at 11.00. He did not summon them as their Senior Officer but as an equal; his signal was headed 'Admiral Commanding Battle Cruisers'. They had come together and considered setting up a committee to interview lower deck representatives, to convey their feelings to the Admiralty, but decided that would be too slow and difficult. They decided instead on the insistent demand for an immediate concession on pay. None of them ever reported that this had taken place (S. Roskill, *Navy Policy Between the Wars*, II, p107, 1976). It was true that the day was not going well in Cromarty Firth.

The men in *York* had met in the night, and decided that they needed to do something to demonstrate their visible solidarity with the other ships. They worked normally until colours were hoisted at eight o'clock, when all ships behaved with the usual formality, and then a crowd of over a hundred men gathered on the forecastle and began cheering. The Captain, afraid of attempting another confrontation between seamen and marines, contented himself with reading the Articles of War to that part of the crew which had fallen in properly for 'Divisions' at 8.45, and asking them to use their influence on their fellows. Petty Officers and Chief Petty Officers, like the Officers of Warrant rank, were cautioned not to do anything that might provoke more trouble. The men were edgy, having been constantly taunted from *Valiant* by shouts of 'Y-O-R-K YELLOW!'

The Captain's address had little effect: as one man put it, 'The Articles of War make you think a bit, but they couldn't hang the lot of us.'

At 9.45 Rear-Admiral Astley-Rushton, in charge of the cruiser squadron, came aboard. He addressed the men, again without result. But as the morning wore on, some of the men began to be frightened by what they were doing.

> I remember feeling, seeing the indiscipline and all that, you know when discipline breaks down and anything could happen – so many men, feeling quite a sense of panic. I remember being quite scared to think that anything could happen. Boats were being lowered and people messing about, communicating and all that sort of thing – and then we heard that the cook had gone on strike, we wasn't going to get any dinner. All that sort of silly talk went on [Lingham].

Gradually they began to return to duty, and by the time the Admiralty were sent the panic signal from the Fleet, the *York*'s forecastle was clear. But the situation was more dangerous in Astley-Rushton's most rebellious cruisers, *Norfolk* and *Adventure*.

He had gone to visit *Norfolk* before coming to *York*, and had made something of a fool of himself. He was an arrogant and bullying man, and he was naturally deeply upset by what had happened. There was some good reason why the battleships and battlecruisers might mutiny – they, after all, had been due to go to sea – but it made no sense for the cruisers to blot their (and his) copy-book. A Royal Naval Volunteer Reserve boy watched his performance with fascination.

> A red-faced admiral came aboard from a picket-boat manned by petty officers and we were summoned to the quarter-deck. This is usually done at the double but the men just sauntered there. The admiral stood on a gun turret and harangued us in an explosive fit of angry words mixed with curses. As a young man I was most shocked to hear an officer cursing (I was a civilian, remember). As he shouted men just drifted back to the forecastle, without permission [D. Stone].

The gist of Astley-Rushton's argument, apart from the information that the crew of the *Norfolk* were fools and hooligans, was that the crew of the *Dorsetshire* had long ago resumed duty, so why didn't they? Although the *Dorsetshire* was only a few hundred yards away, each ship was so isolated that no one believed him. In the event they proved correct – towards one o'clock a crowd began gathering on *Dorsetshire*'s forecastle.

The same correspondent mentions that Astley-Rushton was taking a very different line from that of the Captain of the *Norfolk* – but Captain Prickett was a broken man. His one attempt to restore discipline on his ship had been to go to the forecastle, where a mass of men were listening to records;

> He put his arms around the shoulders of the nearest, and, with tears on his face, made a heartfelt plea to all to resume their duties. It was a most moving moment. The Captain was obviously popular and many must have felt like throwing in the sponge. . .I think he said

how he had always treated them fairly [D. Stone, letters of 4/1/81, 4/3/81].

Astley-Rushton also paid a visit that morning to the *Adventure*. He approached the mid-ships gangway in his motor-boat, but the men lined the rails and began jeering him. They would not let him come aboard. He was having a bad day. Richard Ley, a Royal Marine, was standing idly by the rail: he was Corporal of the Gangway.

> From where I stood on the deck it looked like he was crying. He appealed to everybody to have some common sense and to go back to work and something would be organised. Nobody would take any notice. He was speaking through a megaphone. 'Please, men', or something like that, 'go back to work. We'll get it all sorted out eventually – I know it's hard for you, but this is three hundred years of tradition gone down the drain if you carry on like this.' Really upset about it.

In all the ships there was a growing tension as men began to worry about the lack of response to their action: as some began to waver in their determination, others toured the ships reminding them of their obligations to their comrades. Meanwhile the pressure from some of the more vigorous men for more drastic action was growing. At midday in the *Hood*, two leading seamen reported that they could no longer control their men. It was decided to pipe 'Make and Mend' – a half-holiday. The same device was used on the 'Loyal *Malaya*', where a plan to paint the ship's side was prudently abandoned when ten men failed to turn out in the morning. *Repulse* and *Warspite* also had plans for painting which were abandoned when substantial numbers failed to turn to. *Warspite*'s crew did not entirely down tools, however; they provided a boat for the Captain of *Valiant*, whose own crew refused to man one – as did the crew of *Hood* (letter from H. Fox, written 17 Sept 1931).

In *Valiant*, the only work was being done by officers and

midshipmen. When the ship had been preparing for exercises, sub-calibre firing mechanisms had been fitted to her guns. These cut down the cost of firing by reducing the size of shell required from a hundred pounds to three pounds. If they stayed in place, however, there was a danger of damage to the guns. Peter Dyke, Marine Corporal, remembers seeing the sub-calibres being taken out by the officers.

By this time the industry of the ship had got under way: behind one breakwater you would find a chap soling shoes; the jewing firm, which was the sailor's sewing firm – one with a machine, the button-boy sewing the buttons on, another making buttonholes; then there'd be a photographic firm – a couple would have bought themselves a couple of good cameras and they'd take photos. Each gun was separated off by an armoured wall, and behind each one would be the master of his trade going on. Haircutting, threepence a time. Well this lot got going during the morning, in all the various casemates. In my particular casemate, which was P1, six-inch gun, that was the narrowest one, almost right forrard with a gangway through behind my gun, there was a dartboard. Now the lads were up there, eleven o'clock in the morning, playing darts – which they didn't ought to have been. In the meantime it was decided that these sub-calibres had to come out.

So the gunnery officer, with our gunnery intructor and the midshipmen, started trying to take these out. They were very heavy things, and very difficult to handle. You had to have a big hand-spike in the breech end of it and unscrew it from the main gun, then launch it out and then get on the muzzle and hump it away. And they weighed, oh, I suppose ten hundredweight, half a ton. And these poor little middys, fourteen and fifteen years old, they found it a bit difficult. And the fellers would say 'Look, move your – get out the way of the dartboard – let them get the gun out.' Absolute nonchalance from the troops. And the officers of course realised that they were not held by the tabs, so that they didn't do anything to foment any trouble.'

This, then, was the condition of the Fleet when the Admiralty communicated the results of the Cabinet meeting. The signal they sent indicated that there was a serious intention to alleviate the pay cuts, and that the breach of discipline would be ignored if it now ended.

> The Board of Admiralty is fully alive to the fact that amongst certain classes of rating special hardship will result from the reduction in pay ordered by His Majesty's Government. It is therefore directed that ships of the Atlantic Fleet are to proceed to their Home Ports forthwith to enable personal investigation by Commanders-in-Chief and representatives of Admiralty with a view to necessary alleviation being made. Any further refusals of individuals to carry out orders will be dealt with under the Naval Discipline Act. This signal is to be promulgated to the Fleet forthwith [ADM 178/129].

At about the same time a long signal was sent to Balmoral confirming what had taken place, saying that the Board had no reason to suppose that the Fleet would not sail but adding that they were now engaged in drafting orders to deal with such an emergency if it should arise' (ADM 178/129).

There are absolutely no traces of such orders in the available Public Records, nor, indeed, are there any other references to them. They would make interesting reading. Presumably they are orders to carry out the original plan for a military assault on the Fleet. Such an event would undoutedly have had a profound effect on British political life. The next few hours were to be very tense indeed.

9
Will They Sail?

The order to return to home ports came as a complete surprise to Tomkinson. He had just sent another officer to London with a further batch of sample hardship case-studies, and was fully expecting some sort of concrete offer to be made to the men. He had requested – demanded, even – that a representative of the Admiralty be sent to the Fleet. Three years later Admiral Sir Roger Keyes, Tomkinson's commanding officer for many years, said in the House of Commons

> In these days of quick transport, it would have been quite possible for, say, the First Sea Lord, who by virtue of his office is responsible for the discipline of the Fleet, or other members of the Board, or senior officers whom the Admiralty might have delegated to represent them, to have flown to Invergordon and to have been there within a few hours. After all, the Admiralty were entirely responsible for the situation which had arisen, and they alone had the power to investigate the men's grievances. . . .
>
> On the morning of 16th September, Admiral Tomkinson had every right to expect the support and intervention of the Board of Admiralty. The action he had taken up to date made that intervention quite possible.

At this point we move into an area of real uncertainty in the historical record. According to a substantial number of men present in the Fleet, a very senior officer did make his appearance among them, speaking with an authority which appeared to over-ride both the Board of Admiralty and the

Cabinet. Their account cannot be substantiated from any available records, and it is denied by many others – yet these men insist on it.

There has undoubtedly been concealment of the true story surrounding the 'mutiny'. The whole of the story concerning the preparations to attack the Fleet has been hidden. It is possible that this story too has been carefully expunged from the record. But without a single shred of documentary evidence to support the tale, it cannot be taken as historical fact. It will find its place later in this chapter, and readers must make what they can of it. For the moment, I want to relate the story of Wednesday afternoon as men tell it without bringing in this mysterious messenger.

There is no doubt that every officer in the Fleet understood the importance of persuading the men to accept the order to sail. They did not know of the retribution that might come from the hills if they failed, but they did know that the future of the Navy, and perhaps the nation, now hung in the balance. Tomkinson relayed the signal to the Fleet just after three o'clock, ordering that sailing should begin at nine. There were just under six hours left in which to end the mutiny.

In a small number of ships the order was accepted without demur. In *Repulse* and *York* the order was taken at its face value – but *Repulse* and *York* may perhaps have had special reason for that, as we shall see later.

In *Rodney*, too, it was accepted without question – indeed with positive jubilation. The men were convinced that they had won. But this was not the case in the majority of the Fleet. The original refusal to sail had put the men of the lower-deck in a strong position: they believed that it would be impossible to impose the Naval Discipline Act so long as they all remained together. Once a ship put to sea, however, anything might happen – it might be sent anywhere, and the men on board might be dealt with as mutineers. The object of the Home Ports order was to divide the moderates from the determined activists, but its success would depend on how many men had their homes in those ports. In most ships there were arguments between those who saw the home ports order as a trap, and those who were willing to accept it as a welcome way out. Generally speaking, those who took the latter view were themselves 'natives' of the home port towns, while those who argued against them were 'non-natives', for whom the home ports held less attraction.

In *Adventure*, for example, there was a furious debate, as Ackland recalls. It was still going on when the ship sailed at 8.20.

> 'Fo'c's'lemen on the fo'c's'le – quarter deck men on the quarter deck' sort of thing, and 'Stand by for leaving harbour'. 'Close all portholes and scuttles' and that sort of thing. The officers were on the fo'c's'le – the officers were there, that was the fo'c's'le officer, the officer that was doing the anchors, getting the anchors up; there was two midshipmen; and I think there was a gunnery officer. The men had left the fo'c's'le. They were all discussing this now down in the recreation room. The discussion was 'Shall we or shan't we.' The people that lived in Devonport and Plymouth were all for it – they were going home. But the foreigners, like the Welshmen or the Irishmen, or the Scotsmen, who didn't care two hoots, they wasn't concerned. And actually, the officers worked the cables. The men hadn't arrived at their stations. There was no decision that they shouldn't sail – the discussion was going on whether they would or they wouldn't, and it was so excitable that you couldn't understand what they were going to do. But the officers worked the cables. I was a quarter deck man.

Once the Captain had found that he could get the engine-room working, he had ordered the officers to take the ship to sea.

The officers had got one anchor up when a body of men rushed on to the forecastle to obstruct them. Marine Cor-

poral Ley remembers the next few moments as the tensest
of the mutiny.

> I was walking about on the gangway. The Captain of
> Marines made the remark, in the hearing of several
> ratings, 'Let me fix bayonets, sir, and I will clear the
> decks'. Well as soon as that was heard one of the ratings
> went forrard, told his pals and said, 'Right, let's batten
> the bastards down!'
>
> Now our messdeck had one big hatch coaming. They
> battened that down, and cleated it. But some of us were
> already out. When they saw me walking about, one of
> the ratings said, 'Grab this evil one here and let's chuck
> him overboard! Let's show 'em what we'll do with the
> Marines!'
>
> Well there was a sailor aboard called Johnston who
> lived in Leeds like me, and we were great pals, and he
> said, 'Oh no, no, no; leave him alone. He's a pal of
> mine. He's all right. He's one of the good ones.' And
> they let me go.
>
> This was the only time I'd ever known seamen react
> in a hostile way to Marines. But it wouldn't have hap-
> pened except for the Captain of Marines, who was a
> diehard who was ready to clear the decks regardless of
> consequences. Captain Dibben wasn't as hare brained
> as the Captain of Marines. Clearing the decks would
> have been a bloodthirsty job.'

Once the drama of the moment passed, the men were
readier to accept the order to sail: officers assured them that
they were, indeed, going to their home port of Devonport,
and there seems to have been a growing feeling that they
needed to escape from the situation they were in. *Adventure*
was the first ship to sail.

The Captain's report to the Admiralty makes no mention
of any of this. The ship's log claims that the ship had been
in normal routine ever since the home ports order was read

to the ship's company. Captain Dibben would conceal what he could. Three weeks later he was relieved of his command.

Once the *Adventure* began to move, the other cruisers got under way at five-minute intervals. First was the *Exeter*, in which there had been no trouble; next came Astley-Rushton's flagship, *Dorsetshire*.

Tension had been building in *Dorsetshire* earlier in the day; a crowd assembled on the forecastle in the early afternoon, following continuous barracking from other ships, and began to cheer back. When the home ports order came, the Commander went to the fo'c's'le: the men ran away, but he called them back and read the signal to them. They went below for tea, and copies of the signal were posted in the mess-decks: instead of improving the situation, as Astley-Rushton had been confident it would, the order gave rise to exactly the same kind of debate (though less acrimonious) as in *Adventure*, and it was not until the lower-deck was given the assurances of senior officers that they were not being tricked, that they agreed to sail.

The next ship out was *Norfolk*. Here the suspicions of a trick were also strong, and because of the unusual nature of the mutiny on this ship there was a struggle on the part of the ship's committee to retain control – a struggle which turned to violence. Their control was already weakening, as the resolution of part of the crew was wavering during the day, and this seems to have made them tense. George Hill, the Commander's writer and go-between to the men, was ordered by the Commander to issue sailing orders.

> My first reaction was a common-sense one; I thought the mutiny had been brought to an end and nobody had told me. I felt something of an ass. But he didn't say any more and he turned to leave the office. I called him back, and said to him, 'Excuse me, sir, but what's this all about?' So he then gave me the information that the Admiralty had made a signal ordering the ships to return to their home ports for investigations, and pro-

vided the men returned as ordered there would be no disciplinary action taken against the mutineers. Now that seemed to me ideal, very nice. As he turned to leave again I couldn't help but say to him, 'Has everybody been informed?' To which he replied, 'No. You're going to do that.'

I went on the mess deck and I gave them the message that the Commander had given me. But I made one terrible boob. I immediately followed it up by saying, 'I'm now going back to the office to get out the orders for sailing.' Personally, I felt that everybody would jump at the idea. But a linkman decided otherwise. He quickly told me, 'You'll do nothing of the sort. You'll stay where you are and we'll decide, not you, whether the ship sails.' The linkman then made it clear to the men that in his opinion this was a ruse. Get all the ships to sea, let the Admiral report to Admiralty that the ships are at sea, and we can expect a signal to come back saying, 'The ships are now to remain at sea and act independently.' It was a ruse to break up the mutiny.

I asked Wincott, 'What do you think you'd like to do about it?' He said, 'I agree with what's been said, it could be a ruse. But it's a risk we have got to take.' And with that I thought the matter was at an end. I turned to leave, to go back to the office, when I was told to stand fast once more. 'You think you've won', said the linkman. 'But let me tell you, if this ship doesn't return to Plymouth, neither you nor your bloody typewriter will see Plymouth again, because you'll be thrown overboard.' And with that, a stoker jumped onto the mess table and turned to me again, shaking his fist in anger, red in the face and said, 'Yes, let me make it clear that we' (that's the stokers) 'will supply the firebars and tie 'em to him and make sure that he bloody well sinks.'

In fact the committee had collapsed, and there were a number of fights on board between those who wanted to hold out and those who did not. Gradually the hard-liners found their support ebbing away. Meanwhile the Captain, the Commander and other officers went to the forecastle and asked one man by name if he would return on duty: when he said yes, others sheepishly followed. They had been shouting 'No, No' to *Dorsetshire*; now the men on *Hood* began shouting the same thing to *Norfolk*. But it was nearly eight o'clock, and it was plain that most of the other cruisers were getting ready for sea. The men on *Norfolk* saw no reason why they should be the scapegoats of the squadron. They sailed at nine thirty-five, in their correct position in the line, followed by *York*.

Before the year was out, both the Captain and Commander of *Norfolk* were relieved of their posts. The Captain was shunted off to a tactics course, and the Commander was put on half pay.

With the cruisers gone, that left the battleships and battlecruisers. These included *Nelson*, *Valiant* and *Hood*, three of the four ships whose refusal to sail had been the original basis of the demonstrations (the fourth was *Rodney*, where there was no problem over the home ports order).

In *Valiant*, though the officers had been treated punctiliously, the atmosphere had turned nasty; now that a committee had been formed to present the men's demands to the Admiralty (they hoped), there was a growing similarity with the *Norfolk*. As in the *Norfolk*, the prominent members of the committee were men who had spoken in the canteen, notably AB's Day and Brockway, and a marine, Coleman. Lieutenant-Commander Drage had tried to influence men in the morning by telling them (wrongly) that they were the only ship still on strike; the men explained to him that this was the only effective form of protest they had, that many of them had married on the strength of assurancces that the old pay rate would not be reduced to the level of the new, and that when the police had protested about the May Committee's proposal for a 15 per cent cut in their pay, a wave of protests had led to an actual cut of only five per cent. By the time the home ports order came, Drage noted in his diary, 'we were clearly approaching a crisis'.

Once the order arrived, Captain Scott ordered lower-deck to be cleared, and all crew to assemble on the quarter deck. Including Chiefs and Petty Officers, only about two or three hundred men obeyed; a further group of perhaps two hundred men went to the forecastle. The rest hid. Lieutenant Elkins went to the forecastle, to see the Commander and Lieutenant-Commander Drage addressing the crowd there. 'They were obviously defiant.' When they were given the order to assemble on the quarter deck, confronted by these officers together with the Master-at-Arms and all the Regulating Petty Officers, the crowd responded by staying put and giving three cheers. Elkins felt that the time for decisive action was approaching fast.

> I concluded that things were critical, and went straight aft to the quarter deck, since it seemed that nothing but force would now succeed. I intended to see that the necessary arrangements were made for serving out arms and ammunition [Elkins journal, NMM].

He urged the Captain to speak to the men on the forecastle. Drage, who believed that he and the Commander were having some effect on the men there, was appalled by the Captain's effort when he arrived. Elkins records simply that Captain Scott warned the men against future breaches of discipline and assured them that the home ports order was not a trick and that they would be treated fairly. In Drage's ears this speech was 'a harangue which, if it meant anything at all, was an attempt to lay the blame on the West Country ships. That put the lid on it' (Drage journal). The men cheered defiantly, and the Captain withdrew to the men waiting on the quarter deck. Once there, it appears that Captain Scott ordered the Captain of Marines to clear the forecastle, shooting if necessary. 'The latter asked for the order in writing. The Captain then sent a note to the Admiral asking permission to open fire on the mutineers' (letter of

L.B.D. Kenny, 19/9/31). This is presumably the note referred to by Elkins in his journal, carried by Lieutenant Fenton to Admiral French in *Warspite*, saying 'the ship would be ready to sail to time using force if necessary'. At this point it was noticed that a tell-tale light had gone out over the aft deck sentry's cabin, indicating that someone had opened the door of the small arms magazine. Marine Corporal Dyke remembers the shock of fear of that moment. 'If no keys had been signed for, out of the sentry's log, and he held the keys of everything, then of course there was queries. There was a panic.' Elkins went to check the log, and found that no key had been issued; worse, he learned that the sentry who had been on afternoon watch had gone forward onto the forecastle.

> So the gunner, he straps on a pistol and gets a couple of the gunner's party and they go to investigate this. All the troops are now very expectant on the quarter-deck; what's going to happen? But in the event he came back and they had an electrician with them. The light had gone out on its own. Panic eased [Dyke].

The initiative was now with the officers; the men on the forecastle were not, after all, armed.

> The Captain ordered the bosun's mate to go around and pipe that anybody who was not on the quarter deck within the next five minutes would be in future treated as mutineers. So our Lieutenant, Lumsden, came to me and Corporal George Revel and if you can imagine the scene: the ship's company were lined up as far aft as they could get, because there was about eleven hundred of us aboard there, and the foremost end of the quarter deck was now practically clear, all around X turret. So I was put on the port side and Corporal Revel was put on the starboard side, clear of the now existing body of men down there, to prevent anybody among the late-comers joining up with the main body [Dyke]

Brockway, one of the more prominent figures in the strike, had gone onto the quarter deck; so had Coleman. They were both moved into positions where the men on the forecastle could see that their supposed leaders were no longer with them. Elkins takes up the story.

> All the loyal Marines on the quarter deck had just been ordered below to get arms and ammunition. Lieutenant Ralfs came up and said that as they were so few, he was taking two Lewis guns and wanted the ammunition. I sent the dagger gunner to see about this.* Drage and I then went forward again – to meet the men streaming aft.

A small number remained on the forecastle, and when Drage told them they would be called mutineers, they replied, 'We're *not* mutineers, sir.' They would not, in all conscience, abandon their position until ordered to do so by name; thus relieved of responsibility for their actions, they went aft to join the rest of the ship's company and listen to the Captain's assurance that they would truly be sailing to Chatham, and that they were not being tricked.

The *Valiant* was a strange ship; the officers seem to have lost any sense of loyalty to a crew who could bring them to this state and the ship was paid off prematurely before the end of the year. Drage wrote in his diary that he was 'damned glad to see the last' of her. Elkins told me 'I was very glad to get out of the ship.' She was the only ship apart from *Adventure* to have her commission terminated as a result of the mutiny. But she was by no means the only ship where force was seriously considered to get to sea on Wednesday night; that happened in *Hood* and *Nelson* as well.

In *Nelson*, the home ports order was read just before four in the afternoon, and led to the usual argument over whether or not it was a trick – once more the split tended

---

*It must have been around this time that Admiral French came aboard in response to Captain Scott's note. He told Scott to 'use all persuasion'.

to be between 'natives' and 'non-natives' of the port, in this case Portsmouth. Commander Lake went around talking to groups of men, urging them to obey.

> The men were afraid that as soon as they landed there would be a crowd of pongoes [soldiers] on the jetty to march them all off to jail. Commander Lake said 'I give you my word as an officer and a gentleman that no man will suffer as a result of returning to home port. The matter will be investigated by the C-in-C and you'll all have the chance to tell the C-in-C how you're suffering' [C. H. Williams].

Lake's word was worth a lot in *Nelson*, but the men were also aware that as flagship of the Fleet, other ships would follow their example, and they were afraid that they would be letting the side down by sailing. There were furious discussions in the mess-decks over what to do. At five o'-clock the Captain told Lake that, because of the vital significance of getting *Nelson* to sea, he was prepared if necessary to part the cable. This would have cleared the foredeck by killing or injuring everyone on it, as the cable whipped out at speed. Captain Burges-Watson then went to the *Hood* to tell Tomkinson what he planned to do.

The *Hood* was in a similar condition to *Nelson*. The afternoon's 'Make and Mend' had been interrupted at quarter to five by the Captain clearing lower-deck to tell them of the Admiralty's signal. This was the first time that the Captain had appeared before his crew since the trouble began. His speech was not well received, and he began to adopt a menacing tone.

> The Captain said, when he was on the capstan on the fo'c's'le, 'Of course, we haven't had the Royal Marines up here.' And somebody said. 'You get the bastards up here!' And 'Can you guarantee that we *will* go back to Portsmouth?' And he said, 'I can give you my personal

guarantee that we will be sailing to Portsmouth' [S. Wheat].

The Captain left the forecastle, and the men on it began shouting 'No! No! No!' to the other ships near them.

Captain Burges-Watson of the *Nelson* asked to see Tomkinson, but Tomkinson would not see him – he was, apparently, too busy. One does wonder what was more important at this moment for Tomkinson than helping the Captain of *Nelson* to get his ship to sea. Unfortunately Tomkinson never mentioned Burges-Watson's visit in his Report of Proceedings; neither did Captain Patterson of the *Hood*. It does not even appear in the *Hood*'s log. Evidently everyone had their own ideas about what the Admiralty should be allowed to find out. According to Burges-Watson's report, he saw the Flag Captain instead, and they agreed that both *Hood* and *Nelson* would part their cables if necessary to get to sea.

At seven o'clock, knowing that some ships were in difficulties, a signal was sent by Tomkinson's staff telling those ships who could to sail and not wait for those who could not. Shortly afterwards, Tomkinson signalled to the Admiralty that sailing was due to start at nine-thirty. 'I am not at all sure that all ships will leave as ordered but some will go '

In fact the situation was calming down by the time that signal was sent. In *Nelson*, Lake worked hard on persuading men that any further disobedience would get them into real trouble. Paymaster Lieutenant-Commander Duckworth recorded both sides of the argument in his diary.

> Their attitude was – we are in a strong position here at Invergordon as a fleet – if we go to home ports as ordered we all get split up and can't act together – we're all in this sink or swim together – we in this ship do not want to let others in the fleet down by forsaking them – we don't know what other ships are going to do. . .we have committed ourselves so far, if we alone forsake the others the Admiralty will drop down on us like a ton of bricks and we shall be the victims and

marched off under escort to barracks on arrival in Portsmouth – in fact we don't really know what to do, but we think we'd better stay where we are and work it out and see it through once and for all.

The counter-arguments played on the very fears contained in all this, by interpreting the home ports order.

Admiralty have given you a chance and stressed that 'further' disobedience will be dealt with by Naval Disobedience Act implying that they will overlook matters up to date – therefore don't spoil your chances now – Admiralty have ordered all mails to home ports already – they can stop all your allotments at any moment (a very strong point this) – they can pay you all off up here without being at a home port simply by not paying you anything at all – if you go to Portsmouth the C-in-C will be able to come aboard personally to go into the matter.

These arguments began to have an effect, especially as it became visible at around seven o'clock that the less-affected ships were preparing for sea. Lake then went to the forecastle and addressed the men still there. He stressed that they would go back, not as shameful mutineers, but as the Fleet flagship and the proud winners of the silver chanticleer, Cock of the Fleet. 'He promised us that when we returned to Portsmouth, our own home port, he said they'll put the silver chanticleer in B turret and we'll go up harbour playing Cock o' the North' (C. H. Williams). It worked.

In *Hood*, the same process of gradual collapse was taking place among the 'mutineers'. When it came to preparing for sea, the heart had gone out of them. No orders were piped, in order to avoid giving any public opportunity for mass action against them. Individuals were given orders, and obeyed them as individuals.

At ten-twenty on Wednesday night, the battleships and

battlecruisers began to leave Cromarty Firth. The mutiny was over. But the crisis was just beginning.

Before we can turn to that, however, it is necessary to examine the strange statements made by a number of men in *York* and *Repulse*. They concern Admiral John Kelly, known throughout the Navy as 'Darby' Kelly.

Kelly was a remarkably popular man, with a reputation on the lower-deck for good sense, plain speaking, absolute honesty and impatience with cant at any level. He had many friends in high places, including King George V; he was the man to whom the Navy Secretary, Stanhope, had written that extraordinarily indiscreet letter about the Board of Admiralty early in September. He was in retirement on half-pay at his home in Somerset, hoping for a senior appointment in the near future. According to a large number of men that I have spoken to, John Kelly appeared from nowhere on Wednesday in Cromarty Firth. The most striking accounts come from men in the *York* and *Repulse*. Here, for instance, is a stoker from *York*:

> Now that man – the men in the Navy trusted him. He was definitely a man you could trust. . .He didn't come up the gangway and be piped aboard the same as most Admirals, he came over the boom [i.e. as a sailor would come aboard, and onto the forecastle]. He saw the men that were up there and he came down from the fo'c's'le onto the quarter deck and naturally the pipe went, 'Clear Lower Deck'. So we all mustered on the quarter deck, all except about thirty or forty men that were still on the fo'c's'le, they wouldn't come down. We cleared lower deck to hear what Sir John Kelly had to say.
>
> Anyway, the Captain straight away said to the marine lieutenant, 'Get your men up on the fo'c's'le, I want those men down on the quarter deck!' John Kelly says, 'No! Leave them where they are! If they don't want to hear me, that's OK with me, they'll hear it from the men that are here.'

Now the first words he said to us, he said, 'Now all you officers except the Captain and the First Lieutenant can clear off the quarter deck. I haven't come to speak to you. I've come to speak to the men.' Of course they were flabbergasted, weren't they?

'Now as most of you men know,' he said, 'I've been retired a number of years. But KG5 (which was King George the Fifth) asked me personally to come up and take over the Atlantic Fleet to see what I could do about this so-called mutiny. I know you men have been treated rough,' he said, 'there's quite a few of you here that this really affects. The old rate of pay men. But you 1925 men haven't got nothing to worry about at all. Not really, It doesn't affect you.'. . .He gave us quite a good speech, he explained everything, he said 'I shall do all in my power to get it altered when we get back. What I'm going to do now is disperse the Fleet to home ports, a fortnight's leave for each watch. How's that?'

It was a wise thing to do.

As it stands, this seems an absurdity. Fifty years on, memory becomes blurred, and even if Kelly was there he can hardly have said that he had been asked to take over the Atlantic Fleet – that had definitely not happened. And to claim authority for the home ports order on his own account seems decidedly unlikely – that had been proposed by Admiral Field and backed first by the Board of Admiralty and then by the Cabinet. Kelly was indeed given command of the Atlantic Fleet later – he assumed command on 6 October – and he came aboard each ship after he had been appointed and made a most impressive speech. It seems as though this stoker has simply got muddled.

But there are two more very similar accounts, different in detail but essentially the same, from other men who were in *York* – men from different parts of the country, who have had no contact in the intervening years. One is from an Artificer Chief Petty Officer who took no part in the strike action himself. He says that he clearly remembers Kelly coming aboard and saying to the men that he had been asked by the King

> to go and see what you can do to sort things out. So here I am and this is what I propose to do. I'm sending you to your home ports and giving you leave so that you can go home and work out with your wives how best you can manage. In the meantime Their Lordships at the Admiralty will do what they can to resolve the issue.

When I put this story to all five men I have contacted from *York*, two of them insisted that Kelly did not come aboard. Unfortunately, such evidence is not conclusive either – one of these two, for example, insists that the Captain at no time addressed the ship's company, which is certainly untrue.

I have fewer accounts from *Repulse*, only four, but two of them are remarkably similar to those from *York*: a torpedo-man, for example, says

> The men worshipped Kelly. They really worshipped him. I'd known him in previous years in other ships, when he'd been in charge of various fleets, and he was a typical old sea-dog and he could speak the language of the lower deck. . .
> The gist of his speech was that he totally agreed with us as regards the cuts and what he'd like to do was to go down to the Admiralty and speak on our behalf; and the only way he could do it was if he had his fleet, all the ships, back in their home ports, which would cut out any talk of mutiny or whatever you like to call it. He said, if we do that he'd order the ships back to their home ports, give normal leave and then take himself to the Admiralty and, in his words, 'Take his boots off.'
> All he wanted to do was get back to the Admiralty and fight on our behalf.

Only one of my four contacts from *Repulse* insists that Kelly did not come aboard in Invergordon, but he was a boy of seventeen at the time and would not have known him anyway.

There is a third ship – *Valiant* – from which there are similar accounts, but these only serve to confuse the issue. None of the twelve men from Valiant who were interviewed or corresponded with for this study made mention of him being there, nor do the journals of Drage or Elkins, or contemporary letters that I have seen from the ship. The three accounts which do speak of Kelly appearing in *Valiant* were written in recent years: two of them in letters to Lieutenant (by then Rear-Admiral, and knighted) Robert Elkins, following a television programme on the mutiny in which he took part. Both the letters are friendly greetings from men who took some part in the strike, and who stress that it was not a mutiny; they have plainly remembered Kelly's visit in October and wished it back a month (ELK 10). The same applies to the third such account from *Valiant*, in an article in the January 1975 *Naval Review*, by A. J. Farlow, a Petty Officer Gunner's Mate who served under Elkins. Given the weight of negative evidence concerning Kelly from this ship, perhaps these accounts are evidence of a state of mind; a state of mind in which men want to believe that a figure appeared among them who represented the paternalistic and patriotic spirit of the service, to whom and through whom they could express their strong sense of loyalty. On that reading, the Kelly story might well be seen as an indication of a feeling that they were not mutineers and that in a sense it was the Admiralty who were out of line; their strike was to save the Navy from the Lords of Admiralty, and they have conjured Kelly to give them a hallucinatory benediction.

Perhaps that explains everything. But perhaps not. Farlow's article attracted immediate denials that Kelly was there, and that in itself was surprising. Although Petty Officer Farlow believes that he did see Kelly at Invergordon, his article did not really make that clear: it said simply,

'Subsequently Admiral Kelly came on board and talked to all hands and being the man he was some sort of order was restored.'

The ship was in a state of disarray when it left Invergordon, and it is true that when Kelly came aboard on 13 October his address to the men did restore some sort of moral order. One might have thought that anyone who knew the story would have read the paragraph to refer to that visit – even though that was not the reading intended by the author. It is curious, then, to a suspicious mind, that two letters were published in the following edition of the *Review* specifically picking up this point, stressing that Kelly was not at Invergordon and inviting readers to believe that Farlow was referring to an incident in 1932 – an impossibility, since *Vullunt*'s crew were paid off in December 1931 and she was recommissioned with a new crew.

The accounts of Kelly's appearance in *York* and *Repulse* may also be fantasies, but here they come from a majority of the men, and I have found no contemporary journals from these ships to provide negative evidence. There is no record in the ships' logs of Admiral Kelly coming aboard – but there are many things which logs do not record. A number of the cruiser logs, and *Repulse's* log, make no mention of the mutiny at all! The Captain's reports are equally unreliable documents:

> The reports rendered by Captains of individual ships cannot in every case be relied upon. My own Captain, from what he himself told me, omitted so much and minimised so much else as to give a totally untrue picture of events [Drage, 'Invergordon Reflections', 1933, IWM].

There was no official drama made of Kelly's visit in the Fleet – but he was in retirement, and was not entitled to the protocol rituals accorded to a Flag Admiral. Surely, had he been there, he would have called on Tomkinson? Yes, but then one does wonder what Tomkinson was doing on

Wednesday afternoon, when he was too busy to see the Captain of *Nelson* to discuss the most important problem of his career – how to get *Nelson* to sea? Perhaps he had Kelly on board then. Surely, though, if Kelly was in Somerset, he could not have come to Invergordon in time? Well, he could have travelled on Tuesday from his home to Balmoral, perhaps going part of the way by air – and then comes the question, who was the mysterious Captain S. R. Mallet with whom the King dined on Tuesday night? Army Captains are usually called 'Mr', Naval Captains have RN after their names (Admirals don't). Balmoral is about four hours by road from Invergordon.

Could the home ports order have come via Kelly's advice to the King – or even following an early morning drive from Balmoral to Invergordon? It certainly seems amazing for Field to have had confidence that it would do the trick if the only advice he had was from Tomkinson and Colvin, who were adamant that the Fleet would not move unless the pay cuts were reduced. I have seen nothing in the official record to support such a speculation – but when even the Board of Admiralty apparently kept no minutes of its key meetings, one cannot draw many conclusions from that either.

Perhaps the most puzzling assertion, and the most difficult to explain away, is that Kelly was seen talking to a group of sailors ashore in Invergordon. There were certainly men going ashore on official business – in small numbers – on the Wednesday, and it is possible that with boats going between the ships, some men were getting ashore unofficially as well. Mr Edwin Corbett, who worked behind the bar in the Royal Hotel, Invergordon, and who was thirty-two in 1931, insists that he saw Kelly address a meeting of sailors in the vicinity of the canteen: he had gone down to the pier to see what was happening, heard that the meeting was going on and walked over to find out what he could.

He got a great reception, he was very, very popular –

144

very popular. There was a huge crowd, he was in the centre saying what he was going to do and they protested they wouldn't go to sea. The only way they'd go to sea again was if they went to their home ports. And I remember quite well, he was smoking a cigarette at the time and he couldn't get it lit and he went across and saw a sailor and got a light from the sailor. That was Sir John Kelly. They went back down King Street quite happy – they were going to go home. They were going to their home ports.

There was undoubtedly a crisis of the greatest national importance. There were clearly plans being prepared for marines to be brought into action with artillery against the Fleet. It could just be true that Kelly was employed by the King as a troubleshooter in the greatest secrecy, and that he visited and spoke to men in two ships whose crews were known to have been reliable late on Tuesday – one at the mouth of the Firth, the other in the middle of the Fleet. Ships whose sailing might influence others, and which might, if things turned really nasty, be used against others.

It is an enigma. But so is the whole story of Kelly's appointment to take charge of the Atlantic Fleet a few days later.

10
Phantom Terrors

The Fleet sailed from Invergordon on the night of Wednesday 16 September. Two nights later, as they were steaming South at speed, there was a new alarm.

> *Saturday, September 19th*
> Important developments last night in this ship [*Nelson*] indicated that present trouble is far more serious than I can indicate in this diary. With the enemy in our midst effective action is difficult without giving our knowledge away.

This is an extract from the diary of Lieutenant-Commander Duckworth, Paymaster in the Fleet flagship. By the time he came to write this, on Saturday, he was evidently in a state of panic.

> Quiet conference all evening in and about Commander's cabin. Very difficult to act without arousing suspicion. We are powerless anyway. Any demonstration would further panic the fighting forces of the Crown and be disastrous to the country in present circumstances. Our opponents know this and bank on officers' absolute trust and casual lifelong reliance in accepted methods of discipline, not to sleep with revolvers under our pillow – for example! We cannot afford to underrate the means they will employ to bring pressure. Very few people in this ship realise the gravity of the situation.

The panic seems to have been caused by a cypher signal which was believed to have been sent illicitly from *Rodney*: '*Nelson* will now take over pivotal ship. Keep your end up and do not forget . . . [there follows what may have been a time and date].

It was believed in *Nelson* that this signal indicated that a new outbreak of trouble was intended for Saturday night, but Duckworth recorded that 'Later C-in-C Portsmouth got a correct version of message showing this to be Tuesday 0800.'

The mutiny had broken the morale of many officers. The sudden realisation that discipline and authority depended on consent had shaken and cracked the solid ground on which they stood. Duckworth's diary neatly demonstrates the stages which led to the panic which followed.

On Thursday, the day after the mutiny ended, he wrote his immediate thoughts:

> The terrible feature of the situation is the realisation by all – for ever – that discipline only works on the surface. Given a bad enough situation and force of numbers will always win. Twenty officers can't 'make' a thousand do something if they decide they don't want to. There may be no ill feeling, but if a thousand say no, there is no human way for twenty insisting on yes, and the Naval Discipline Act goes overboard. If it goes overboard once what is to prevent it going again when opportunity offers and who can stop it?

This was a perception shared by the world's Press. The *New York Times* had come out on Wednesday morning with a report that

> There is fear among Government officials tonight [Tuesday] that the trouble will spread to the army and the police forces, which were also subject to heavy wage cuts. . . . It is very evident that there is fear of trouble with the police and soldiers, even the school teachers, because of the pay cuts. . . . The country has been flooded with propaganda denouncing the pay economies as needless and as something dictated by Amer-

ican and French bankers . . . it has been feared there
would be disturbances on the part of the unemployed.

National government, as well as naval discipline, depended on consent and the 'disturbances' were taken as a
sign that such consent was lacking. In Germany, the Communist newspaper the *Red Flag* published a telegram to 'the
English sailors in revolt', calling for revolution and the formation of sailors' soviets. The German government, believing that it needed to assist Britain's evidently delicate
stability, suspended the paper's right to publish.

The way the mutiny ended, with the government agreeing
that sympathetic treatment should be given to hardship
cases, was generally taken as confirmation of a surrender to
force.

> As startling as was the incipient mutiny in the British
> Fleet [wrote the *New York Times* on Thursday] the action
> of the government in making terms with those who
> have broken discipline is regarded as even more
> startling. . . .
>
> Not only have British seamen refused to obey orders
> thereby forcing the postponement of manoeuvres of the
> Atlantic Fleet, but they have set an example of disobedi-
> ence to other services civil and military.

The government, however, was not prepared to accept
that it had surrendered. Chamberlain's statement to the
House on Wednesday afternoon had actually committed it
to nothing.

> Personal investigation will . . . be made by the
> Commanders-in-Chief and representatives of the
> Admiralty into those classes in which it is alleged that
> the reductions press exceptionally on those concerned.
>
> His Majesty's Government have authorised the Board
> of Admiralty to make proposals for alleviating the hard-
> ship in those classes as soon as the facts have been
> ascertained by the contemplated investigation.

It was still for the investigation to prove that the men had a case and for the government to agree any concrete remedies. There were, it was true, cheers from the Labour benches and cries of 'You've surrendered once and you'll keep on surrendering,' but that was not the government view. They knew that they had to prevent their foreign creditors from taking fright, and therefore persuaded themselves that they could still get out of this without making definite concessions. Once the men had a chance to cool off, it was believed, they would settle down to the new pay scales – with, perhaps, the possibility of an extra charitable fund being created for married men under twenty-five who were in real difficulties.

The King himself, who had been so anxious to have this budget accepted that he had created the National Government for the purpose, shared in this wishful thinking.

> The King feels, as everyone else does, that there is nothing wrong with the men but that they were taken by surprise before full explanations could be made to them. The statement issued from the Admiralty last night put the whole thing in a better perspective, and showed that there was no question of a twenty-five per cent cut [Wigram to Chetwode, 17 September, ADM 178/129].

The Admiralty sent a signal to be read to all ships' companies in the Fleet, telling them off and urging them to behave better in future.

> The Lords Commissioners of the Admiralty view with the gravest concern the injury which the prestige of the British Navy has suffered due to the recent behaviour of the men of the Atlantic Fleet. The Board rely on the personnel of the Fleet to do their utmost to restore the confidence of the Country by their future behaviour, particularly during this period of national crisis.

Given the state of morale of the officers, this cannot have

been an easy document to read aloud on any of the ships. Duckworth's diary indicates the mood.

> Reflections of the situation and press news received show that the seriousness of the matter is still not realised by Admiralty. References in Parliament etc. to Their Lordships 'trying to find a method of investigation with a view to etc . . .' quite beside the mark. Admiralty have *got* to give way or trouble will be worse. Therefore economy can only be met by reducing expenditure on fuel and *ammunition*. This should have been done in the first place and the money saved without touching the individual's pocket. They now bleat about 10% reduction of ammunition allowance *'if it can be carried out without serious dislocation of firing programmes already arranged'*!! As if any practice mattered 2d. at this juncture. We are dominated by the fleet-action type of mind which believes war, and a fleet action to be expected next week. Utter nonsense these days – yet we go firing away millions of money in useless target practice. We're no better now after 15 years than we were at Jutland and still can't *hit* anything deliberately. Cut it all out – and with it all the Dreyers and Astley-Rushtons.
>
> I think S.O.A.F. should point out to Admiralty now – this afternoon – that they *must* give in, and the sooner the less trouble – too late to talk about enquiries and 'trying to *find* methods of alleviation'; not to waste time consulting the Cabinet who don't care a pin *how* the Admiralty economise so long as they do. If one plan won't work, another must be tried.
>
> Shouldn't be surprised if there isn't a public enquiry into why this has all happened at all and whole Board of Admiralty resigns. [Duckworth, Diary, Friday 18 September].

The hostility to 'the Dreyers and Astley-Rushtons' is perhaps a reflection of the resentment felt by many non-military officers at their own exclusion from command. He was

wrong in supposing that there would now be a public enquiry. There would not even be any Courts Martial. Austen
Chamberlain had made that clear in Parliament, to the as-
tonishment of the rest of the Board. He had been confronted
on Thursday evening with the news that a major run on
gold had begun. To stem the tide, he decided to draw a line
under the mutiny; it was over, and everything would now
return to normal. He publicly commended the way Tomkinson had handled the situation, and went on to say,

> The past is past. It is in the interest of everyone in the
> Navy and out of it to forget it. I am not going to look
> back . . . there will be no looking back to what has
> happened on this occasion, but we shall go forward
> together in the service of the country.

This statement was positively frightening to many officers.
It meant that the men responsible for the mutiny could not
be weeded out and punished. Signals between the Admiralty and Tomkinson form a numbered sequence, and five
signals in that sequence, transmitted the morning before
Chamberlain made his 'forgive and forget' statement, are
missing from the public record. Since there are no signals
on record concerning disciplinary action, it may be that
these concern the Courts Martial which were not now to
be permitted.

'Every person subject to this Act shall suffer death, or
such punishment as is hereinafter mentioned.' The Naval
Discipline Act had now truly gone overboard, thanks to the
First Lord. If one believes, as every lower-deck man who
talked to me believes, that the mutiny was a spontaneous
eruption against the prospect of intolerable hardship, that
is a very good thing. But many officers had formed a more
sinister view. There were a number of Captains who were
convinced that the mutiny had been planned before the
autumn cruise began, that there were agitators at work in
Invergordon who had links with some men in the Fleet
(who were those civilians in the canteen?). The evident feel-

ing among many Chief and Petty Officers that the strike was justified, and their unwillingness to take a strong line against it, reinforced their fear. For those who had always viewed the lower deck as 'the lower orders' it was hard to believe that the mutiny of so many ships could be arranged by the men themselves; easier to accept that it was the work of plotters, manipulating the men. Somehow that belief combined with the officers' loss of confidence in their own authority, and their fear of the evident insensitivity of the Admiralty and government, to produce a phantom conspiracy.

> Very few people in this ship realise the gravity of the situation. Their aim is to further shake confidence in the country at all costs, push the cart downhill faster and faster whatever happens, the sailors and their grievances being used as pawns in the game during the first stage – and quite likely ignorant of the real significance of their actions.

That was Duckworth's analysis of the supposed message from *Rodney*. Invergordon was evidently only the curtain-raiser; worse, much worse, was still to come.

The atmosphere on board most ships had been, inevitably, rather strained on the voyage back to home ports: while hardship investigations were continuing, lists were also being compiled of men who were considered to be most deeply implicated in the mutiny – 'ringleaders'. In *Valiant*, one seaman came to Drage and 'confessed' to having organised the mutiny in that ship, a claim which Drage ascribed to vanity, but which he nevertheless believed. In most if not all ships, men who were known to be 'loyal' were asked to report on the activities of these suspects. Arthurs, a torpedoman in *Dorsetshire*, was one of those picked out for this duty. 'The Commander sent for me and he asked me to observe the ringleaders and what they were doing and pass on to him any information that I could get. I had no option.'

Sometimes these informers were discovered by the men: Hiscox, in *Rodney*, found one.

> Everyone was looking over his shoulder for informers. We found one, me and a friend. We said, 'Right, now we'll inform on you.' We did him up with stolen stuff, in his locker, in his kit, in his pockets, everywhere. He went to prison.'

There was a general atmosphere of nervousness. As the ships approached their home ports, ships' companies were warned to keep their mouths shut about what had happened. The Press would be out in force, and they should say as little as possible.

By midday on Saturday all the ships involved, with the exception of *Warspite*, *Exeter* and *Malaya*, had docked and their crews had been given leave for the weekend. The three exceptions, ships least affected by the troubles, came back a little more slowly, with the result that their crews had less leave than the others. This did not go down terribly well with them. Jack Hooper, a Marine in *Malaya*, was astonished to find that his ship was evidently being less kindly treated than those which had defaulted.

> We were given extra weekend leave for loyalty – hip, hip, hurray. Now I used to use a sailor's club in Plymouth which we used to call The Free State. I had a locker there with civilian clothes in. So I go in, change into civilians and up into the restaurant part, and usual, egg and chips – and I spotted a Marine that had joined up with me and was in the *Norfolk*. So I gathered me eggs and chips and I went over and said, 'What are you doing here?', like, and he says, 'Oh, I'm on a long weekend. What about you?' I says, 'I'm on a long weekend *for loyalty*.' Of course there was a little bit of chat and one thing and another. And I thought, 'Well, that's all right! I get a weekend for loyalty, he gets a weekend for chucking his hand in. Where do we go from here?'

The men had come ashore in Devonport to find the local papers full of lurid accounts of their doings, and were depressed by a general atmosphere of dismay that they had broken faith with the nation. They also found the pubs and clubs in all the home ports full of secret service agents.

> An old mess-mate of mine had left the Navy and I met him ashore in a pub, and he was in there in uniform. I was curious. He sat alongside me in the pub and told me then he was in the police – he'd been put back into uniform to find people who were trying to stir up trouble, civilians [C. Cloake, A. B., *Rodney*].

The intelligence agents were being given plenty to work on. *Hood* had raced back at speed to dock at six-thirty on Saturday morning, with Nelson just half-an-hour behind her. Duckworth persuaded the Captain of *Nelson* to let him dash over to Tomkinson as soon as the ship arrived in harbour, carrying a telegram already cyphered for the Senior Officer to send to the Director of Naval Intelligence warning of the 'plot' for 0800 Tuesday morning 'and for him to ring up Duty Commander Admiralty and get him busy'. Duckworth left *Nelson* at Spithead in a motor-boat, so that he was already waiting in Portsmouth Harbour when the *Hood* came in. He was prevented from seeing Tomkinson by Admiral Colvin, who had just returned from the Admiralty to the *Hood*, and who seems to have mistrusted Duckworth's information. 'He turned down the idea of telegraphing to gain two hours, alleged Admiralty had matter in hand. I seriously doubt this' (Duckworth, Diary).

Tomkinson himself did not mention any 'plot' in his Report of Proceedings. He knew perfectly well how the mutiny at Invergordon had come about. The story was, however, taken seriously in Plymouth, where it was 'confirmed' by the Commander-in-Chief. Naval Intelligence there was led a dance in the pubs on Saturday night by unhappy and mischievous sailors. Bassett, the intelligence officer who had been sent to Invergordon, had heard an exciting tale there of Len Wincott's skill in organising mutiny. Bassett had also, not surprisingly, felt that Wincott's Machiavellian role was confirmed by the *Norfolk*'s 'petition'. Now Bassett was in Devonport, listening to stories of a plot to catch buses and trains from the home ports to London. 'It smacked of the master hand of Len Wincott.' He telephoned the Admiralty on Sunday evening, and was told to come up to Whitehall at once.

In Whitehall, panic reigned. The change of atmosphere in the Admiralty can be timed fairly accurately: on Friday afternoon Tomkinson had signalled that he proposed to go straight from the *Hood* to the Admiralty, arriving early Saturday morning: he had received a reply from Admiral Field, the First Sea Lord, indicating that the Admiralty really had no need of him. 'Although I shall be glad to see you at any time I suggest you remain at Portsmouth so far as necessary to assist C-in-C Portsmouth in his investigations.'

That message was timed at 16.17. Two hours later, at 18.15, the First Sea Lord changed his mind. 'PERSONAL IMMEDIATE. Please cancel my 1617. I shall be very glad to see you tomorrow, Saturday, please telegraph your time of arrival when known.'

This was presumably the effect of new information, the information which had so frightened Duckworth. Meanwhile a different sort of information was beginning a panic in the Cabinet.

Thursday's attempt to calm foreign fears about unrest in the Navy had failed; in a world in which international currency markets were highly unstable, Invergordon had started an avalanche. On Thursday, £10 million had been lost; a further £18 million in gold was withdrawn from the Bank of England on Friday. The foreign loan of £80 million which had been secured by pushing through the budget was evaporating hour by hour. An approach was made to Paris and New York for new funds. It was turned down. Just before ten o'clock on Friday night, Ramsay MacDonald was told by the Bank of England that there was no alternative to the unthinkable: the Gold Standard must be abandoned.

On Saturday morning, when Tomkinson came to the Admiralty with his own report and those of his Captains, when Naval Intelligence was receiving its first 'confirmation' of the continuing plot, the Directors of the Bank of England wrote to the Chancellor and Prime Minister with a formal request to cease exchanging sterling for gold.

> If the Gold Standard goes, the trade of the world would be plunged into a welter of depreciating currencies. . .Revolution will follow in Central Europe, leading possibly to the triumph of international Communism.

That was what the government had been formed to avoid. Now, it seemed, they had failed. The Cabinet Secretary's diary for Sunday indicates the frame of mind in which the government approached the fateful public announcement.

> On Saturday morning I was very busy on the Bank Holiday proclamations – a most complicated business. [These were a precaution against a panic run on the banks.] But, for fear of creating a panic, it was necessary to keep quiet that we were taking these powers. If the King had been in London it would have been easy to have the necessary instruments ready and to summon a Privy Council meeting at short notice to pass them. But the King was [at] Balmoral. The lawyers would not let us have a Proclamation with the date left blank. So, as we could not tell on what date a panic might arise, if it does arise, we had to get the King to sign five separate Proclamations proclaiming a Bank Holiday, i.e. one for each day Monday to Friday. Privy Councillors had to be collected from places within reach of Balmoral, and elaborate arrangements made for secrecy. The Council is fixed for 4p.m. this afternoon. Clive Wigram, who has succeeded Stamfordham as [the King's] private

secretary, was very cool, and I fixed the whole thing up by telephone. I also looked into our food supply, which appears satisfactory and into the national strike organisation, as we cannot foretell what will happen. I had a long talk with the P.M. in the morning, and we lunched together at the U.S. Club. He showed good courage after the prolonged strain. I told him that in the war, whenever we met disaster, we tried to get some good out of it [S. Roskill, *Hankey, Man of Secrets*, 1972, II, pp. 558–9].

And still the information was coming in to the Admiralty that an uprising was planned for Tuesday morning. Bassett's telephone call on Sunday night came after the Board of Admiralty had spent the day in 'almost constant session' – a session of which there are apparently no minutes. In the early hours of Sunday morning the situation had been made even more alarming by the news that a sympathetic strike had taken place in HMS *Delhi*, in the West Indies.

On Monday morning, when Bassett arrived in London, a stunned nation was faced with the emergency announcement that its sacrifices had been in vain ('Britain Off Gold Standard – No Need for Alarm' *Daily Herald*). Bassett was introduced to an officer from Chatham with similar news to his own, and together they were taken to the Prime Minister at 9 a.m. At 11.30, when the Cabinet's main concern should have been the Bill that was being rushed through Parliament to release the Bank of England from its obligation to sell gold, they were gathered to listen to Austen Chamberlain's assessment of the situation in the home ports. The Director of Naval Intelligence also made a report. Hankey made a record of the main points.

All reports agreed that the situation was extremely serious. There was a complete organisation on the lower deck to resist the pay cuts, and the petty officers were now affected. . .

During the meeting information was received of a

press report from Hong Kong, where some unrest was reported. . .

The men thought that the civil population of the ports was with them, but it was doubtful whether this was the case, at Plymouth at any rate. . .the Communists were active in the ports and had sent some of their best agents there. . .The whole organisation of the lower deck was extremely thorough. The officers of the Fleet considered it essential to limit the cuts ~~to a basic rate of 10%~~ on basic rate to 10%. ~~On the whole the officers were sympathetic with the grievances of the men, but of course did not countenance their methods of ventilating them~~ The officers undoubtedly sympathised with the grievances of the men, though doing their best to restrain them. [Deletions as in the original].

Sir Austen Chamberlain had enquired what would happen if the gates were closed at the dockyard ports. He was informed that the marines afloat were implicated and that the marines at the home ports were not to be trusted. If the men were allowed to leave the dockyard and then the gates were closed against them there would probably be serious trouble and they might batter down the gates. He had seen the Sea Lords that morning and their recommendation was that the Government ought to announce that as the result of enquiry the cuts should not be greater than 10%. Whether that would be accepted now he could not say [CAB 23/90B].

The Cabinet was thus faced with apparently concrete evidence that the Invergordon mutiny was intended to be an event to be compared with the Russian naval mutiny of March 1917, or the Kiel mutiny of 1918 – the beginning of the end for the established order. The budget was no longer important – the battle for the Gold Standard had already been lost. It was now a question of survival. If altering the pay cuts could do any good, then they must be altered. A few days later, Chamberlain wrote

> I was in fact prepared to tell the Cabinet that I could not remain First Lord unless they granted our requests; but I never use language of this kind till it has become absolutely necessary and on this occasion they accepted my view even before I had finished the exposition of my case [Letter of 3 October, Sir Charles Petrie, *Life of Sir Austen Chamberlain*, 1940, II, p 384].

The Cabinet had certainly good reason to be fearful of the consequences of a mass eruption in the home ports. The political mood of the country was tense enough before Monday's announcement about gold; on Friday, Aneurin Bevan had apparently warned Parliament that the Labour Party was ready to join in unconstitutional action.

> If this Committee imagines for a moment that we are going to confine ourselves to sterile Parliamentary opposition at a time when they are making use of the most ruthless class policy that this House has ever carried out, if they think that we are going to repeat the docility of 1921–1929, they really must think that all the guts have gone out of Englishmen. . .As far as we are concerned there is one thing about which we are pleased in the present crisis, and that is that the change over of this party from there to here has clearly exposed the class issue. We shall carry it through to a final conclusion, be the circumstances what they may.

The prospect that all this inflammatory rhetoric might produce real action was genuinely frightening now that the nation had stepped into the abyss. The Cabinet authorised the Admiralty to restrict the cuts to a maximum of 10 per cent, a decision which was communicated to the House of Commons that afternoon, and relayed to all Commanders-in-Chief.

The government waited to see what would happen on

Tuesday morning. The King had been kept informed of the supposed threat; an indication of the scale of anxiety is contained in the opening words of a letter from Chetwode, Chamberlain's Naval Secretary, to Wigram at Balmoral for the King's information. It explained that the letter was being sent in case telephone contact became impossible.

There was no trouble on Tuesday morning. There never had been any prospect of trouble. Not a single man in the lower-deck, out of over a hundred whom I have contacted, knew anything about a plot. There was no plot, no organisation, no threat. The mutiny at Invergordon had created a monster in the minds of officers of the Fleet, and that monster had achieved more, for the men, than the mutiny itself.

It also gave them a new Commander-in-Chief: Admiral John 'Darby' Kelly.

11
Aftermath

Remove grievances, punish ringleaders severely, be
lenient to the rest.

> Lieutenant-Commander C. Drage,
> 'Some Modern Naval Mutinies', Conclusion

The first mention of Kelly taking over the Atlantic Fleet
comes in Duckworth's diary on Sunday 20 September, when
the fear of an insurrection is strong among the staff in *Nelson*.

> The first step is to get a new C-in-C here, Hodges is
> very ill and will be away till Christmas. Tomkinson (he
> would) regards any new C-in-C as a reflection on him
> at this stage. Absurd, his feelings are of no account at
> this initial stage. Believe Secretary Goldsmith is working
> for this as Chief of Staff and Captain of Fleet can't move
> having heard Tomkinson views. . .
>
> We can do so little from *Nelson*, huge staff and no
> Admiral. Suggestion is for Kelly to come here – alone
> – this is no moment to change round staffs – we want
> the one man with all the stripes to take direct control
> – a soviet of Rear-Admirals can't handle the situation.

The steps by which Kelly came to be appointed seem to be
a secret still. There is every reason to believe that he was
placed in command on the personal insistence of King
George V, to defuse the crisis and sort out the Atlantic Fleet.
That was certainly the rumour in the Fleet, and it is supported by the memoirs of Lord Davidson. Davidson had
been Naval Secretary in 1924–6, and had formed a great

admiration for Kelly; he was also a close friend of the King. The emergency plans that were being dusted off in the weekend after Invergordon, in case of a general strike or insurrection, had been drawn up by Davidson in the 1920s, and since he was still an elder statesman of the party (and would indeed return to Cabinet office, again in charge of emergency planning, in October) it is likely that Hankey would have turned to him that weekend for advice. Davidson was clear about the need for strong authority at such moments:

> The Government has the duty to protect the people against any attempt at direct action by revolutionary measures to put in an anti-democratic body to control the country. . .An attempt to substitute an oligarchy with no claim to represent the majority of the people had to be resisted at all costs.

He was certainly well informed about events inside the Admiralty that weekend. On Monday, Chetwode drew up a memorandum for Field outlining possible replacements for Hodges, and recommending that while the best choice seemed Tyrwhitt (then Commander in Chief Nore), there would be no need to appoint 'the best man' unless the Fleet failed to come to order. In the normal course of events, Dreyer would take over the Fleet in 1932, and before deciding to upset that, Chetwode recommended, the Board should leave Tomkinson in command and see how things developed.

Davidson was firmly of the opinion that only two men, Kelly and Tyrwhitt, could restore order in the Fleet, and since Tyrwhitt was in poor health (a fact not mentioned by Chetwode), it would have to be Kelly. He quickly discovered, however, that Field and Chamberlain shared Chetwode's views. Davidson later wrote,

> I made my views known to the Court and also drew Stanley Baldwin's attention to the situation. As a result,

the Cabinet overruled the choice of the First Lord and insisted that Kelly should be given the command.

Commander Kenneth Edwards wrote in 1937

> It is widely believed among naval officers that the appointment of Admiral Sir John Kelly was not only constitutionally approved by His Majesty King George V, but was definitely made by him in defiance of intrigues for the command which had been prosecuted within the Admiralty [*The Mutiny at Invergordon*, p. 372].

Dreyer, in his letter to the Secretary of the Board, trying to kill the book, said that this was 'pure invention – utter rubbish' (DRYR 8/1). Since the post was originally to have been Dreyer's, however, it is unlikely that he would have been kept in the picture while these decisions were being taken.

Kelly was summoned by telegram on Wednesday 23 September, and when he arrived at the Admiralty next day he was offered the post. It is curious that neither the telegram, nor the letter offering the post, have found their way into the Admiralty files (the originals are in the Kelly papers, KEL/109) – but then, there is no document indicating that anyone in the Admiralty ever gave serious consideration to offering Kelly the post. It is clear, however, from the documents that are available for the next few days, that the King had demanded a full accounting. Chamberlain sent His Majesty a letter of apology for not having given a personal account of what had taken place, and stressing that it was 'in no sense communistic or a revolution'.

The draft of this document, which shows the hand of Dreyer, blames the urgency of Cabinet decisions and the refusal of the Cabinet to allow the Admiralty to provide early warning to the men, ahead of the budget.

In this week, too, the Admiralty began preparing a 'Narrative of Events' for the King. It took more than a month of drafting and redrafting to produce an acceptable document

– that is to say, one which did not seek to lay the blame on the Cabinet, but which also contained nothing which might 'cause a wrong impression that the whole matter did not receive at each stage the fullest consideration of the Board, as a Board', or which might suggest that the Board had at any stage stampeded the Cabinet. (Principles set out in a memorandum of 21 October by C. B. Cornwall.) This involved a very far-going series of evasions and omissions: there can be no doubt that the original pay cuts were made without the Board as a whole considering or even knowing that they were being made, that there was deep resentment in the Board at the fact the Navy cuts had been more severe than those in other areas (where more careful recommendations had been made to the new Cabinet), and that they made full use of the hysteria on the 21st to hustle the Cabinet into accepting a revision of the cuts. The final version of the Admiralty Narrative was a document which can only be described as deliberately misleading.

The King, however, did not depend on the Admiralty for his information. He asked Kelly to draw up his own report of the Fleet – a report which was requested by the Board, but which was delivered first to the King. The King also told the Admiralty that he expected to be given detailed information on the movements of the Fleet. (Telegram 15 October, Admiralty to Commander in Chief, Atlantic Fleet, ADM 178/110.)

Kelly, the man the men could trust, naturally wanted to begin with a clean slate, and to have troublemakers out of the Fleet before he took command. For that reason he put off his appointment until 6 October; he saw the King three days earlier. He gave the Admiralty a list of officers that he wanted removed, and saw to it that Naval Intelligence took a hundred and twenty seamen, stokers and marines from their ships into shore barracks. The majority of these were Devonport men. 'They promised no recriminations. What a joke!' That bitter comment is from a marine in *Valiant*. *Valiant* lost thirty men – more than any other ship. Once in barracks, these men were subjected to a 'training' course which amounted to a series of punishment drills – especially at Devonport – and were kept under constant surveillance. The marines were marched off *Rodney* and their sergeant was publicly stripped to a private. 'It was pathetic. We cheered them as they went ashore.'

In many cases the men who were discharged to barracks had taken only a slight part in the mutiny – they were simply men who had come to the notice of the officers. Two of the men whom Arthurs in *Dorsetshire* had reported as 'ringleaders' were picked out apparently on the basis of the information he gave. Bert Fordham in *Nelson* shared a gun-turret with a man who had apparently been of no prominence whatever, but who was suddenly ordered out of the ship. William Symons, whose name had been taken when he refused to go on deck, was one of the men ordered into barracks from *Nelson*. So were the man who fell overboard returning to *York* on Monday night, the man who played the piano on *Rodney*, a man from *Nelson* who was overheard saying that the mutiny had been a good thing. Only in *Norfolk*, where the leadership had been real and evident, were there 'ringleaders' to be sent ashore, and eight men were picked out including Wincott and Copeman.

According to the Navy's rationalisation, these men were not being punished for what had happened at Invergordon; they could not be, Parliament had been told that would not happen. If they were to be punished at all, it must be for their part in the agitation for a renewal of the mutiny, the agitation which had panicked the Admiralty and the Cabinet into limiting the pay cuts to ten per cent. On 13 October a report from the Director of Naval Intelligence admitted that there was no evidence of serious plotting at Portsmouth or Chatham, but stated that of the 38 Devonport men who had been initially discharged to barracks, 12 were implicated 'in the subversive plot which was being hatched at Plymouth during the weekend 20th September.' These men were given no opportunity to clear themselves – they were not even told of the accusation. It was a charge for which there was no acceptable evidence, since there had been no agitation.

By the middle of the month the number of men discharged to barracks from the Atlantic Fleet had risen to the full 120, and Naval Intelligence reported on 29 October that it could find no evidence of subversive activity on the part of 93 of them: so far as the remaining 27 were concerned, 'the evidence is not, such as, by its nature, can be divulged in proceedings under the Naval Discipline Act.'

With the financial problem now solved – though not in the way intended – a general election had been called for 28 October, and a decision was taken to leave the 'subversives' in barracks until the election was over in order to avoid the political embarrassment of too obviously breaking Chamberlain's pledge. There was undoubted nervousness at the effect of being seen to break the promised amnesty; when Wincott complained forcefully at the punishment drills being inflicted at Devonport, they were stopped. But as soon as the election was over, at least 120 men from the Atlantic Fleet began to be discharged. They were hustled outside the dockyard gates with 13s. and a rail warrant. Among them were, of course, Wincott and Copeman. Some of the men were seen crying outside the dockyard at Devonport. They were reduced to beggary.

The Communist Party was the only place where some of these men could find any succour, and thus the legend of a Communist plot received spurious confirmation. Wincott was their greatest catch; he became a professional propagandist, and today lives in Moscow – despising the 'Establishment' which saw his concern for his fellow-sailors as subversion, but sad at the refusal of the British authorities to allow him ever to make a permanent return to Britain. Copeman found a dockyard job, but Wincott had a letter sent to him at his place of work and he was fired when he was handed the envelope with its incriminating Communist Party insignia. He too ended up in the party: he fought in the International Brigade in the Spanish Civil War. Later he was to play a significant role in organising civilian protection against air-raids in London, and was decorated; he went on to become a popular Trade Union organiser.

The vast majority were simply men the Navy wanted to get rid of; altogether almost four hundred men were sent into barracks from ships around the world in October, as Commanders-in-Chief were given a general directive to remove those 'whose conduct, character or lack of ability renders them undesirable for retention in the service'. Homosexuals, 'lower deck lawyers', anyone who had proved a nuisance could now be dismissed in a general clear-out without any recompense. A great many lives were shattered.

The Atlantic Fleet men who were kept in barracks but not discharged 'Services No Longer Required' were kept under more-or-less constant surveillance, and given unpleasant tasks such as barracks rat-catching. Some were dispatched to distant stations – then moved somewhere else in the world after a week – then moved again after a week – then left to rot for a while in China. Others, whose time was nearly up, were simply kept 'on ice' until they could be removed by the passage of time. Symons was coming to the end of his first term of service and wanted to re-engage for pension: he was kept waiting in barracks until the very hour at which he was due to re-engage, and then told to get out.

The *Adventure* was paid off in November; her Captain had been removed, on Kelly's instructions, early in October. *Valiant* was paid off in December, and her Captain and Commander were sent on courses.

Meanwhile Kelly was restoring the morale of his Fleet. Once the 120 'trouble-makers' had been removed, in mid-October, the Fleet sailed North again, to Rosyth. King George was firmly opposed to returning to Invergordon, and he was obeyed. (Note from Field on a letter from Colvin, 3/11/31, ADM 178/110.) There he went from ship to ship addressing the men. It was an address which few of them have forgotten to this day. Most of the men I have met can repeat parts of his speech word for word. It combined jokes against the Admiralty with compassion for themselves and with a firm authority that was closer to that of a Leading Hand, ready to thump a miscreant round the ear, than that of a well-bred gentleman. Kelly had, after all, been boxing champion of the Fleet and he was generally agreed to be 'a bit of a soft-soaper'. Everyone who served under him has a story about 'Darby' Kelly: how he would wander round the barracks dressed like a tramp; how he would board a ship and detach himself from his official party to surprise the men 'secretly' polishing brasswork ahead of them: how he would ask sailors for a light. Hubert Fox, a midshipman in *Warspite*, wrote a letter home describing Kelly's speech on board.

> He said that two or three months ago the Admiralty had said to him in so many words, 'Sorry, old bean, but we don't want you any more.' He said he turned round and said – then, 'Well, on second thoughts perhaps I'd better not tell you what I said.'
> . . .He told us that he had been talking for two hours to the King before taking up his command. Among other things, the King showed him that his mind was still completely naval and that he understood sailors as well as anyone. He was heartbroken over the recent unrest. Admiral Kelly then explained that the sailors were absolutely loyal to H.M.'s person and crown, as well as to their officers, but he honestly thought that they had been tried too hard – a sailor, he said, did not mind any hardship, death, or anything else, but if his wife and family were tampered with he put his foot down [Letter, 13 October 1931].

Kelly was winning the hearts of the men, for this was a Navy which could only be governed by consent. That was the lesson of Invergordon; a lesson which had deeply shaken the officers, and which had led Tomkinson to report that his fleet had been for two days in a state of open mutiny.

Tomkinson's report has been much challenged: there were few ships which refused to carry out harbour routines after the first few hours of Tuesday morning, and that was all that was required of any of them. The men themselves, of course, still insist that there never was any mutiny – only a 'strike', or 'passive resistance'. But the truth, as everyone in the Fleet knew, was that there were orders which could not be given, because they would not have been obeyed. Even the Admiralty order to return to home ports, which apparently brought an end to the mutiny, was a matter for debate and consent, rather than blind obedience. Individuals obeyed a direct order to return to duty when they were given one, but until it was evident that the lower-deck community as a whole would accept the order to sail such a direct order could not be given. The basic nature of command had changed.

'All governments derive their just powers from the consent of the governed.' That declaration, from the revolutionary American Declaration of Independence, had been working its way through the fabric of Western society since 1776. By 1931 it was well understood in Britain to be the basis of civil government. The achievement of Invergordon was to demonstrate that the same truth now applied to military authority.

> The mutiny did good. It made them see they had intelligent people in the Navy, who were not going to be trampled on [Sam Wheat, Leading Seaman, HMS *Hood*].

> Naval morale was improved by the mutiny – you could have a voice, not just knuckle under [Robert Brown, Chief Petty Officer, HMS *York*].

> We felt it was good. The strike altered the Admiralty's view of the lower deck. Conditions improved after that [Buck Donovan, Stoker First Class, HMS *Rodney*].

> It proved they can't push a serviceman about; he's got

his rights the same as an ordinary workman [Interview 34, anonymous AB, HMS *Valiant*].

The effect of revising the pay cuts was actually very slight. There were very few men who were on the old rate of pay without allowances – the men who would have born a cut of 25 per cent had the original cuts gone through. The basic rationalisation of bitterness had been the plight of married men on the old rate of pay, but in fact only 4 per cent of the cruiser crews, for example, were married, on the old rate of pay, and ineligible for marriage allowance – about sixty men. A special fund was set up to help them. The men who were bearing the greatest percentage cut were those with no allowances – men on the old rate of pay who had not qualified as specialists and who had forfeited their good-conduct badges. These were the men who benefited most from the restriction of the cuts to 10 per cent of basic pay. For the majority of men, subsequent cuts in allowances brought the total loss of pay close to that originally ordered.

In the months which followed there was a long and wretched argument within the Navy over who should be blamed for what had happened. Field and Dreyer insisted that the blame could not be said to rest with the Admiralty: not only would that be bad for naval morale, but it was not true. Blame, they insisted, lay at one extreme with the Cabinet, who had treated the Navy unfairly, and at the other with the officers and Petty Officers of the Atlantic Fleet. Kelly laid some of the blame on the Petty Officers, but was deeply impressed by the officers' hostility to the Admiralty, and particularly to the civilian element there – a hostility which had been re-inforced by confrontation with Admiralty representatives at the brief enquiries into hardships which had taken place in the home ports. Kelly and the King both shared the view that ultimate responsibility for what had happened lay with a weak and incompetent Board of Admiralty, but the Board itself succeeded in deflecting the real penalties onto the men who had been in command – particularly Tomkinson, Astley-Rushton and the Captains of *Adventure, Norfolk, Repulse, Rodney* and *Valiant*.

Dreyer, the Deputy Chief of Naval Staff, led the defence of the Board. He insisted in voluminous and aggressive memoranda that the whole blame really rested on the Cabinet, firstly for not implementing the full May Committee cuts on the police and teachers while imposing them on the Services and secondly, for insisting that notice of the cuts should not be released until after the Budget. It was an argument he maintained to the end of his life.

> To put it plainly, we were left to bear the brunt while *the first National Government, who had made all the trouble by not taking the strongly worded advice of the Admiralty, and by concealing from the latter the fact that they were acting against the Admiralty advice, boomed along with their sails well filled* [F. Dreyer, *The Sea Heritage*, 1955].

This certainly makes it plain why the Admiralty was prepared to use the story of a 'plot' to frighten the Government. Anyone might think that the Admiralty had told the Cabinet not to implement the May Committee cuts. If only they had.

Perhaps the cowardice of the Board is best illustrated in this area by the way Tomkinson was treated: having been spoken of warmly by Chamberlain in Parliament, and having been sent a letter of congratulations for the way he had handled the disturbances from Field, he was given a new appointment and then secretly relieved of his command. The first he knew of what had happened was when he read it in the Press.

A conference of the Commanders-in-Chief of the home ports had recommended that Tomkinson should be relieved only if the Board accepted part of the blame for what had happened. Dreyer, sneering at the suggestion in Kenneth Edwards's book that the Board should have resigned, wrote 'we were made of better stuff than that.' Two other recommendations of that conference were, however, accepted:

the Second Sea Lord was removed, and Dreyer was prevented from ever taking command of the Atlantic Fleet.

Perhaps typically, Dreyer wrote in his autobiography that 'The shabby action of the first National Government' had cost him the job, 'which deprived me of subsequent chances of promotion'.

The sad irony is that a mutiny which did so much harm to the lives of more lowly individuals, and achieved relatively little in terms of the average sailor's pay, did so much good for the country, and for the Navy. Britain had been rescued from its obsession with the Gold Standard and no terrible results followed. On the contrary, the resulting fall in the value of the pound actually strengthened the economy. In the 1920s the application of 'monetarist' policies had helped to make the British economy one of the weakest in the industrial world, but Britain was able to endure the dreadful years of the 1930s without suffering nearly as badly as Germany or the United States. The depression years were bad, but they were far worse and far more deeply disruptive of society in those countries.

Meanwhile within the Navy there was a marked change of attitude towards the lower-deck. Welfare was taken more seriously and physical conditions improved, but, above all, it was recognised that men had to be led, not driven. The lash had long gone, the press-gang had gone even longer, but the intellectual heritage of the wooden man-o'-war persisted in the Royal Navy until the officers had their confidence in command shaken by the wholly peaceful, good-natured and responsible strike at Invergordon.

Perhaps the last word should go to John Gosling, the boy whose experiences started this book; the boy who was taken utterly by surprise when he called the men in *Valiant* to get up on Tuesday morning, and they refused. 'The mutiny was one of the finest things that happened to the Royal Navy.' It's only a shame that the Navy still cannot believe it.

Sources

National Maritime Museum

Papers of Admiral Sir John Kelly: KEL/108, 109, 110, 111, 113.
Papers of Vice-Admiral Sir Robert Elkins: ELK/2, 10, 11.
Papers of Admiral Sir William Fisher: FHR/14, 15.
Papers of Admiral Sir Alfred Ernie Chatfield: CHT/2/2, CHT/3/1, CHT/4/1, 2, 4, 5, 6, 7, 11.
Papers of Commander Harold Pursey: Pursey/10, 11, 12, 13, 14, 15.

Public Record Office

CAB 23/68, 24/223, 23/90B.
ADM 1/8747/78, 87.
ADM 53/70081, 7715, 76044, 78927, 73061, 84906, 85274, 87358, 80288, 81245, 81351, 82565, 88623, 91740, 94203, 83061–3, 74291.
ADM 116/2864, 2884, 3611.
ADM 167/83, 84, 85, 86, 87.
ADM 179/92.
ADM 182/61, 62, 90, 91.
ADM 230/1.
ADM 178/73, 75, 79, 80, 89, 110, 111, 112, 113, 114, 129, 133, 135, 149, 150, 151, 162, 164.

Imperial War Museum

Papers of Lieutenant-Commander Duckworth.
Papers of Commander Drage.
Letter from Lieutenant L. B. D. Kenny.
Transcript of recording by A. B. A. Copeman.

Sources

Churchill College, Cambridge

Papers of Vice-Admiral F. Dreyer: DRYR 3/2, 8/1, 8/2.
Papers of Captain S. Roskill: ROSK 7/171, 172, ROSK 21/3, 3A.
Papers of Captain Godfrey-Fausset: BGGF 1/89, 91, 102.
Papers of Vice-Admiral W. Tomkinson.
Papers of Captain Henderson.
Papers of A. B. L. Wincott.

The Naval Review

January 1975, 'The Invergordon Affair', A. J. C. Farlow.
April 1975, letters from C. C. H. H. and J. S. S. Litchfield.
April 1976, 'Invergordon, First Hand-Last Word?' H. Pursey.
July 1976, letter from C. H. Herdman.

Secondary sources

L. Wincott, *The Spirit of Invergordon*, 1931.
L. Wincott, *Invergordon Mutineer*, 1974.
Commander J. H. Owen, *Mutiny in the Royal Navy*, typescript in
ADM 178/135.
K. Edwards, *The Mutiny at Invergordon*, 1937.
D. Divine, *Mutiny at Invergordon*, 1970.
A. Copeman, *Reason in Revolt*, 1948.
B. Duncan, *Invergordon '31*, 1965.
T. Wintringham, *Mutiny*, 1936.
S. Roskill, *Naval Policy Between the Wars*, vol. 2, 1976.
A. Carew, 'The Invergordon Mutiny, 1931: Long-term causes,
    organisation and leadership', *International Review of Social
    History*.

Personal communications

The following men who were in the Atlantic Fleet have provided substantial information for this study:

HMS Adventure
H. Ackland   Able Seaman
R. P. Ley   Royal Marine, Corporal

Sources

HMS Courageous
L. I. Johnson — Stoker, 1st Class
A. H. Osterloh — L A C (Fleet Air Arm)

HMS Dorsetshire
H. R. Arthurs — Leading torpedo operator
W. A. Gardiner — Able Seaman

HMS Exeter
H. R. Beale — Chief Petty Officer, artificer
F. E. Butler — Stoker, 1st Class
A. J. Deacon — Torpedo operator

HMS Hood
N. S. Carr — Stoker, 1st Class
W. R. Hargreaves — Stoker, 2nd Class
W. Ludlow — Telegraphist
H. Prestage — Ordinary Seaman, RNVR
N. Wesbroom — Ordinary Seaman
S. G. Wheat — Leading Seaman
C. E. Wild — Stoker, 2nd Class

HMS Malaya
S. F. Atkins — Ship's postman
E. J. R. Godwin — Leading torpedo operator
J. V. Hooper — Royal Marine

HMS Nelson
G. A. Ballard — Stoker Petty Officer
W. P. Butcher — Stoker, 1st Class
A. Dobbing — Leading Seaman
A. Fordham — Royal Marine
R. H. Harbin — Stoker, 1st Class
G. Seadridge — Leading Stoker
W. F. Skelton — Cadet
R. Smither — Able Seaman
W. S. Symons — Able Seaman
W. H. Weeks — Able Seaman
A. W. Williams — Signal Boy
C. H. Williams — Ordinary Seaman

HMS Norfolk

C. Boulton	Stoker, 1st Class
A. Copeman	Able Seaman
G. Hill	Commander's Writer
D. Stone	Ordinary Seaman, RNVR
W. P. Wood	Boy Seaman

HMS Repulse

E. F. Eldred	Able Seaman
Mr. Maindonald	Able Seaman
H. L. Morris	Signal Boy
D. E. Pemberton	Stoker, 1st Class

HMS Rodney

C. Cloake	Able Seaman
J. Donovan	Stoker, 1st Class
E. Harris	Ordinary Seaman
T. R. Hiscox	Boy Seaman
J. H. Sampson	Boy Seaman

HMS Valiant

E. Baines	Chief Petty Officer, artificer
C. Drage	Lieutenant-Commander, Signals Officer
P. J. Dyke	Royal Marine, Corporal
C. H. Edwards	Able Seaman
R. Elkins	Lieutenant-Commander, Gunnery Officer
J. Gosling	Boy Seaman
A. J. Jacobs	Able Seaman
H. Masters	Royal Marine
J. T. Preston	Able Seaman
W. Rich	Royal Marine
R. B. White	Leading Seaman
Interview 34, anonymous	Able Seaman

HMS Warspite

N. Clements	Royal Marine
Mr Crosby	Able Seaman
H. Fox	Midshipman
J. Freeth	Able Seaman
R. O. Hunneybell	Royal Marine
R. A. Tyler	Commander's Writer

Sources

HMS York

R. Brown	Chief Petty Officer, Artificer
W. W. Knight	
E. C. Lingham	Telegraphist
H. E. Marris	Able Seaman
W. C. Powell	Chief Petty Officer, Artificer
J. Townsend	Stoker, 1st Class
D. Whiteside	Able Seaman

Index

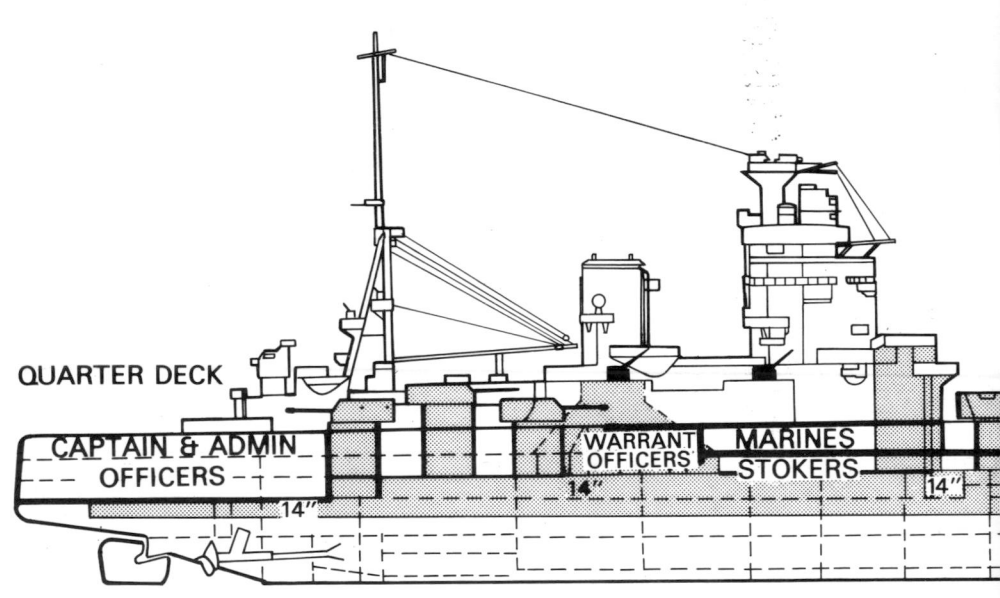

QUARTER DECK

CAPTAIN & ADMIN
OFFICERS

14"

WARRANT
OFFICERS

14"

MARINES
STOKERS

14"

NELSON